Why I Am Not a Feminist

Why I Am Not a Feminist

A Feminist Manifesto

Jessa Crispin

MELVILLE HOUSE

BROOKLYN • LONDON

Why I Am Not a Feminist

First Melville House Printing: February 2017

Melville House Publishing   8 Blackstock Mews
46 John Street   and   Islington
Brooklyn, NY 11201   London N4 2BT

mhpbooks.com   facebook.com/mhpbooks   @melvillehouse

Library of Congress Cataloging-in-Publication Data
Names: Crispin, Jessa, author.
Title: Why I am not a feminist : a feminist manifesto / Jessa
    Crispin.
Description: Brooklyn : Melville House Publishing, [2016]
Identifiers: LCCN 2016032467 (print) | LCCN 2016047106
    (ebook) | ISBN 9781612196015 (paperback) | ISBN
    9781612196022 (ebook)
Subjects: LCSH: Feminism.
Classification: LCC HQ1155 .C756 2016 (print) | LCC HQ1155
    (ebook) | DDC 305.42—dc23
LC record available at https://lccn.loc.gov/2016032467

Design by Jo Anne Metsch

Printed in the United States of America
3   5   7   9   10   8   6   4

A book should open old wounds, even inflict new ones. A book should be a *danger*.

—E. M. CIORAN

Contents

Introduction

Are you a feminist?

Do you believe women are human beings and deserve to be treated as such? That women deserve all the same rights and liberties bestowed upon men? If so, then you are a feminist, or so all the feminists keep insisting.

Despite the simplicity and obviousness of the dictionary definition of feminism, and despite years of working at feminist non-profits and decades of advocacy, I am disowning the label. If you asked me today if I am a feminist I would not only say no, I would say no with a sneer.

Don't worry—this is not where I insist I am not a feminist because I am afraid of being mistaken for one of those hairy-legged, angry, man-hating feminists that are drawn up like bogeymen by

men and women alike. Nor will I now reassure
you of my approachability, my reasonable nature,
my heteronormativity, my love of men and my
sexual availability—despite the fact that this dis-
claimer appears to be a prerequisite for all feminist writing published in the last fifteen years.

If anything, that pose—I am harmless, I am
toothless, you can fuck me—is why I find myself
rejecting the feminist label: All these bad feminists, all these Talmudic "can you be a feminist
and still have a bikini wax?" discussions. All
these reassurances to their (male) audiences that
they don't want too much, won't go too far—"We
don't know what Andrea Dworkin was on about
either! Trust us." All these feminists giving blow-
jobs like it's missionary work.

Somewhere along the way toward female liberation, it was decided that the most effective
method was for feminism to become universal.
But instead of shaping a world and a philosophy
that would become attractive to the masses, a
world based on fairness and community and exchange, it was feminism itself that would have to
be rebranded and remarketed for contemporary
men and women.

They forgot that for something to be uni-
versally accepted, it must become as banal, as
non-threatening and ineffective as possible.

Hence the pose. People don't like change, and so feminism must be as close to the status quo—with minor modifications—in order to recruit large numbers.

In other words, it has to become entirely pointless.

Radical change is scary. It's terrifying, actually. And the feminism I support is a full-on revolution. Where women are not simply *allowed* to participate in the world as it already exists—an inherently corrupt world, designed by a patriarchy to subjugate and control and destroy all challengers—but are actively able to re-shape it. Where women do not simply knock on the doors of churches, of governments, of capitalist marketplaces and politely ask for admittance, but create their own religious systems, governments, and economies. My feminism is not one of incremental change, revealed in the end to be The Same As Ever, But More So. It is a cleansing fire.

Asking for a system that was built for the express purpose of oppression to "um, please stop oppressing me?" is nonsense work. The only task worth doing is fully dismantling and replacing that system.

This is why I cannot associate myself with a feminism that focuses dementedly on "self-empowerment," whose goals include not the full destruction of corporate culture but merely a higher percentage of female CEOs and military officers, a feminism that requires no thought, no discomfort, and no real change.

If feminism is universal, if it is something that all women and men can "get on board" with, then it is not for me.

If feminism is nothing more than personal gain disguised as political progress, then it is not for me.

If by declaring myself a feminist I must reassure you that I am not angry, that I pose no threat, then feminism is definitely not for me.

I am angry. And I do pose a threat.

Feminism is:

- a narcissistic reflexive thought process: I define myself as feminist, so everything I do is a feminist act, no matter how banal or regressive—i.e., no matter what I do, I am a hero.
- a fight to allow women to participate equally in the oppression of the powerless and the poor
- a method of shaming and silencing anyone who disagrees with you, inspired by a naive belief that disagreement or conflict is abuse
- a protective system utilizing trigger warnings, politically correct language, mob rule, and straw man arguments to prevent a person from ever feeling uncomfortable or challenged
- an attack dog posing as a kitten with a droplet of fresh milk on her nose
- a decade-long conversation about which television show is a good television show and which television show is a bad television show
- a bland, reworked brand of soda, focus group tested for universal palatability and inoffensiveness, scientifically proven to leach calcium from your bones, with an

enormous marketing budget; tagline: "Go ahead, be a monster. You deserve it."

- aspiration. Those below you may be pitiable, but not really your concern. Those above you are models of behavior for attaining the best life. The best life is defined as a life of wealth, comfort, and firm buttocks.
- all about you.

For these reasons and more, *I am not a feminist.*

Why I Am Not a Feminist

1

The Problem with Universal Feminism

Every woman should be a feminist." You hear this a lot now, online, in magazines, in conversation. And the thing is, these advocates of universal feminism insist, you probably already are! If you believe women should receive equal pay for equal work and have the right to make their own medical and family planning decisions, then you actually already are a feminist and you should "reclaim" the word.

The idea of universal feminism has entered popular culture like never before, after decades of female celebrities trying to distance themselves from the label so as not to appear unfriendly and unmarketable. The tide has turned. What was unfashionable has now become very fashionable. What was unmarketable is now a marketing strategy. Celebrities, musicians, actresses all proudly proclaim the word. It's in our fashion magazines, it's on our television shows, it's in our music. Feminism is trending.

So we know that we should all be calling ourselves feminists now. What's less clear is what exactly that accomplishes. Or even what, once we do reclaim the label, using the word, buying the appropriate t-shirts (like the $220 scarf from Acne Studios that reads "RADICAL FEMINIST," or maybe the $650 sweater that says the same) and wearing them proudly in public, what exactly are we supposed to do then? And who, dare I ask, are we supposed to be taking the word back *from*?

Is it men who ruined the word for us? They spent a lot of time twisting the word around into an insult, creating panics about feminazi witches causing the downfall of society and conjuring up hurricanes and earthquakes from God's wrath. No, it turns out having a right-wing preacher fling the word at you, trying to make you feel ashamed, just makes you prouder to accept it.

Instead, today women are asking women to reclaim the word *feminist* from other women. Today's feminists accuse the actual feminists of ruining the movement's good name and putting other women off from joining the cause.

Feminism was always a fringe culture, a small group of activists and radicals and weirdos who forced society to move toward them. It was not an overwhelming majority of women who became suffragettes, chaining themselves to fences, going on hunger strikes, breaking windows and throwing bombs. The overwhelming majority of women either didn't care or wished the others would stop making such a fuss. It wasn't an overwhelming majority of women who created a public life for women, organizing women-owned banks and businesses, creating a network of safe (though still illegal) abortion providers, fighting for women's spaces in educational systems, and writing radical texts and manifestos. The overwhelming majority of women during the second wave just wanted a comfortable (married) life with a little more independence.

It was always a small number of radical, heavily invested women who did the hard work of dragging women's position forward, usually through shocking acts and words. The majority of women benefited from the work of these few, while often trying to disassociate themselves from them.

But now there is a different dynamic between the radicals and the mainstream. Now the mainstream wants to claim the radical space for itself while simultaneously denying the work the radicals do. I hear the word *feminazi* coming from young feminists' mouths today way more often than I have ever heard it coming from the mouths of right-wing men. And they're using it in a similar way, to shame and disassociate themselves from the activists and revolutionaries. The most prominent feminist writers right now have twisted themselves in knots trying to distance themselves from their predecessors, willfully misrepresenting the work of women like Andrea Dworkin and Catherine MacKinnon and denying any association therewith. Dworkin's "weaponised shame," Laurie Penny wrote in a column at *New Statesman* without explaining how she has come to sum up Dworkin's belief system as such, "has no place in any feminism I subscribe to."

In order to make feminism palatable to everyone, they have to make sure no one is made uncomfortable by feminism's goals; so the women who advocated for radical societal change are out. Making people uncomfortable was feminism's whole point. In order for a person, or society, to make drastic changes, there has to be a mental or emotional cataclysm. One has to feel, strongly, the need for change before change will willingly be made. And a feminism where everyone is comfortable is a feminism where everyone is working for their own self-interest, rather than the interest of the whole. So, while feminism has become fashionable, the actual feminist work of creating a more equal society is as unfashionable as it has ever been.

Making feminism a universal pursuit might look like a good thing—or at the very least a neutral thing—but in truth it progresses, and I think accelerates, a process that has been detrimental to the feminist movement: the shift of focus from society to the individual. What was once collective action and a shared vision for how women might work and live in the world has become identity politics, a focus on individual history and achievement, and an unwillingness to share space with people with different opinions, worldviews, and histories. It has separated us out into smaller and smaller groups until we are left all by ourselves, with our concern and our energy directed inward instead of outward.

You might wonder, as you read your way through contemporary feminist literature: Why the emphasis on claiming the label? If a woman believes that she is deserving of equal pay for equal work, if she is pro-choice and votes accordingly, why should we care at all whether or not she self-identifies as a feminist?

There are legitimate reasons why a woman, even a woman who believes strongly in equality, would be reluctant to don the identity of feminist. Feminism has had its bleak moments—from the blind racism of some of its leaders, to feminists' siding with Christian leaders in its anti-pornography campaign—and some women understandably have difficulty reconciling these failures with the value of the movement as a whole.

But instead of listening to why you are perhaps reluctant to adopt the identity of feminist, universal feminists, in their efforts to convert, will tell you what your reasons are. You must think, they insist, that all feminists are lesbians, don't shave their legs, hate men, and refuse to become wives or mothers. You must think that in order to be a feminist you have to shave your head, make arts and crafts with your menstrual blood, and listen to folk music. They think the reason you have shied away from feminism is because of feminism's image problem, and the source of this image problem is the radical feminists of the second wave.

If the goal is universality, then these feminists need to simplify the message to such a degree that the only people who would disagree with their pitch are religious freaks and hardcore misogynists. They don't seem to realize that this simplification of feminism into something soft and Disneyfied is one reason women turn away. And look, I get it, all you feminist missionaries. It is disappointing to find ourselves where we are. We are more than a hundred years into this revolution and it's not just that the world remains resistant to women being in it (and it is). Women still face disproportionate amounts of discrimination and violence, and they somehow carry both the burden and the blame for that. If you get raped, it's probably your fault. If you find yourself in an abusive relationship, it's probably your fault. If you get passed up for promotion while male colleagues advance again and again, it's probably your fault. And it's not just that sexual assault rates remain high and prosecutorial success rates remain low, or that what society still values most about women are who they mothered and who they married rather than what they actually contributed to the world.

It is also that so many women themselves are resistant to embracing their own liberation, and in so being, seem to frustrate our own plans for progress.

Some women do refuse to call themselves feminist because the word is alienating to men. Women are still choosing to opt out of work and stay at home to raise children, and women are still taking pole-dancing classes, saying it is good exercise. Women are still painfully removing all of the hair from their bodies and pretending to be morons so as not to threaten their male suitors. They are still giving their money and attention to musicians who tell them they are worthless pieces of ass, now open your mouth bitch and take my dick. Women are still watching blockbuster films and aspiring to be the supportive wife or the sexy girlfriend who needs rescuing, rather than the one (man) saving the world. Women in Hollywood are still producing films where men save the world. They still love and support and marry wife-beaters, rapists, and misogynistic trolls. Women are still voting Republican.

What to do about our reluctant sisters? Many feminists think the answer is converting them to the feminist cause. And the first (and often last in the new age of shallow feminism) step in that conversion is accepting the label and identity. Rather than, you know, showing them that the world and their role in it is fucked.

First, we should acknowledge *why* it is important that women identify as feminist. I mean, important to feminists, not to the world. This has nothing to do with how women choose to live their lives or conduct themselves at work or with their families and communities. With feminism's new focus on labels and identity, rather than on the philosophical and political content of the movement, what becomes most important are the things on the surface. Like using the right words, rather than the wrong words. (The fact that the right words keep changing does nothing to quell the anger that builds in Internet Feminism if you use the wrong words.) This is what happens when simply calling yourself a feminist can suddenly be counted as a radical act.

You see this regularly on feminist blogs and pseudo-feminist-friendly sites like *BuzzFeed*: lists of famous women who refuse to call themselves feminists. These women are listed periodically so that good feminists, properly labeled and identified, can ruefully shake their heads about the other women's ignorance. In the comments, feminists will—instead of reading each woman's reasoning for refusing the label, or understanding the different cultural contexts that older or international women might be coming from— use this public shaming to feel better about their own correct way of thinking and speaking and labeling. *Bust* magazine, back when it was a more outwardly feminist publication, used to ask each of their female interview subjects whether or not they identified as feminist. In 2005, the musician Björk said no, and that interview is still

used in these online lists as of this year. Björk
is a female artist often credited with being one
of the most innovative and daring musicians
of her generation, regardless of gender. She has
collaborated with and supported women musicians, fashion designers, video directors. She has
spoken frankly and openly in interviews about
the difficulties of being a woman in a male-
dominated industry. She has proven herself to
be an exemplary human being and creator, and
she is a tremendous role model for young aspiring musicians. If we understand that the problem
feminists have with Björk has nothing to do with
her actions and is only about her language and
way of identifying herself, then we can recognize
that this is about a feminist marketing campaign
and not a philosophy.

Compare her to the shiny pop stars who have
discovered the market for feminist girl power
and who use the word loudly while displaying regressive ideas, images, and messages. The word
feminist acts as a shield from criticism, and many
of these women are celebrated as heroes. If you
use the proper word, then all is forgiven. You get
a free pass. If you do not use the proper word, this
overshadows all the good work you have done in
your life.

Why is the label, then, so important, if it is

not about putting more interesting, complicated, brilliant women into the world? In a word:
comfort.

If you are surrounded by people who agree
with you, you do not have to do much thinking.
If you are surrounded by people who identify
themselves the same way you do, you do not have
to work at constructing a unique identity. If you
are surrounded by people who behave the same
way you do, you do not have to question your
own choices.

How do we come by new feminists, then, if that
is what we need? Two ways. The first is by re-
branding. Make feminism less threatening and
more palatable. Create a way of showing women
that no matter how they live their lives, they are
already feminists, all they need to do is change
their own labels.

In order to do this, we have to kill the dominant idea about what feminism is—and the
image we all carry around about what feminism
looks like comes to us from the second wave. It's
a lot of anger, a lot of body hair. In rejecting this
version and refusing to put it into context, feminism helps to erase its own radical past. By try-

ing to distance themselves from the bra-burning, hairy-armpitted bogeywoman, they disown and forget all the good this generation of women did. It is therefore important to state publicly, as many current feminist writers have, that at certain points feminism "went too far." All those scary women like Andrea Dworkin and Catherine MacKinnon, Shulamith Firestone and Germaine Greer—who are condemned by this younger generation of feminists much more often than they are read—become scapegoats as their work is willfully misunderstood and misrepresented in an attempt to convince readers and potential feminists of the universal feminists' reasonableness. You can, they insist, still be a feminist and shave your legs, fuck men, consume misogynistic culture. Look, we're doing it, we call ourselves feminists, you can too.

Next, create a friendlier version of feminism where political and sociological understanding of the pressures under which women attempt to live their lives is replaced with personal choice. For example, everything about our culture may be pushing women toward marriage—from romantic narratives in movies and television to health insurance policies and tax benefits granted by the government. And marriage has historically been a way to control women and reduce them to being property—the visuals in marriage ceremonies and the words of wife and husband are still heavy with this symbolic meaning. Yet, if you want to get married and you choose to get married, and you identify as feminist, then your getting married is automatically a feminist act.

Once feminism is transformed from a system with which we can interrogate our societies, our relationships, and our own lives, and imagine and create new ways of being, into a method of self-empowerment and self-improvement, then feminism can become universal. Almost any action or any person can now be labeled as feminist.

The second way to increase feminist ranks is to convince women that their lives will be better if they call themselves feminists. In this way, feminism becomes just another self-help system, another voice telling women they should be having better orgasms, making more money, increasing their happiness quotient, wielding more power in their homes and workplaces. The goal here is self-empowerment, a word that many feminists toss around these days. The ability to live a life of one's own choosing, without any focus on what that life could or should be.

Self-help culture necessarily removes the individual from the societal context in which she lives. We decided to think about our problems in a psychological context rather than a sociological context so that we could at least feel some modicum of control. In this mode, you alone are responsible for your happiness and that happiness is within your control. Self-help culture is also a culture of anxiety. There is always an area of your life that could be improved, and one easily falls into a state of constant assessment and comparison. How is my sex life? I thought it was okay, but this person's sex life seems way better. I wonder if a similar sex life would make me happier. I wonder what she did that I am not doing, how do I make myself deserving of that sex life, she has thinner thighs, if I had thinner thighs I bet I could finally feel really uninhibited in bed.

Women and men who fall into the trap of the self-help mindset spend their time working on their "faults," their weak points, in order to live their best possible lives. Feminism in the self-help mode becomes, then, just another metric to measure, just another process of assessment. So we have books called *Sexy Feminism*, scientific studies about whether feminists have a more satisfying sex or romantic life, personal essays about how feminism helped me get that promotion/ have better orgasms. And while there is a vague notion that there is something called the Patriarchy keeping you down, there are few ideas of how to counteract it, except through individual achievement.

Now that we have removed all meaning from the word *feminism*, our ranks have swelled. We automatically (presto chango) have created an egalitarian society, right? Things have improved all the way around, not just for women but for all people, right?

Converting women to feminism under these conditions does not result in a more fair society or a safer world for women. It is often supposed that acceptance of the feminist label will also result in the acceptance of the meaning behind it, but the meaning has been drained away by this psychotic marketing campaign. A woman can now take up the feminist label without any true political, personal, or relational adaptations whatsoever. It's just another button on her jacket, another sticker on her bumper. The inner contents remain unchanged. All this proselytizing begins to resemble the Christians trying to convert the pagans. ("Really? You have a fertility-related spring festival centered around the egg, the symbol of new life and the powers of procreation? That's so funny, *us too*.") It does not just soothe the minds of feminists who are experiencing doubt. It also keeps the movement as a whole from questioning why women may not want to associate themselves with it.

If feminism really did make women happier and give them better orgasms and stronger marriages and more money, then the proselytizing would be unnecessary. The fact that it does not do these things, by the way, does not speak poorly of feminism.

Breaking away from the value system and goals of the dominant culture is always going to be a dramatic, and inconvenient, act. Surface-level feminism—feminism that requires only a swapping out of labels and no real reform—requires nothing so strenuous from you. To understand how surface-level contemporary feminism really is, we need only note that the most common markers of feminism's success are the same markers of success in patriarchal capitalism. Namely, money and power. Our metric is how many women are the CEOs of Fortune 500 companies, how many bylines at *The New York Times* are women's, what percentage of medical school graduates are women.

We assume the patriarchy will automatically be dismantled if we just manage to get all women to call themselves feminist. A woman CEO can proudly stand up and proclaim her belief in feminism—after all, it got her to this position of power—while still outsourcing her company's labor to factories where women and children work in slave-like conditions, while still poisoning the atmosphere and water supplies with toxic run-off, and while paying her female employees disproportionately low salaries.

Worse than any of that, however, is the tendency of contemporary feminism to see women in power as an inherent good, women like Hillary Rodham Clinton (who, as a senator, dismantled social welfare programs to the severe detriment of poor women and children, as well as supported international interventions that resulted in the deaths and suffering of thousands of innocent civilians), GM CEO Mary T. Barra (who oversaw the cover-up of the safety issues of her company's products, which led to more than a dozen deaths), and other prominent women whose behavior feminists would be condemning if only their genders were different. Women who conduct themselves as ruthlessly and thoughtlessly as their male peers are not heroes, they are not role models. They may call themselves feminists, getting themselves a free pass by many, but that does not mean they should be celebrated.

This is what happens when feminism gets

hollowed out: anyone feels free to take up the mantle, and terrible things are done in its name. What needs to be restored, and can be restored, is a feminist philosophy, and new ideas of what it means to be moral, what it means to participate in the world, and what it means not simply to destroy something, but to build something new.

2

Women Do Not Have to Be Feminists

There is a tendency to look at women who have rejected feminism and decide they must be pitiable. Poor silly cows, they don't know what's best for them. Choosing dependency and subjugation, choosing sad lives of imprisonment and enslavement. When will they awake from their slumber?

It's always going to be easier to pity someone for making different choices than you than to try to understand why they made the choices they did. Otherwise you might have to question your own choices and deal with the possible regret of not having chosen differently. You proselytize to rid yourself of doubt, not to spread the good news.

We speak for these women instead of listening to them. This must be their character: they must be lazy, deluded, greedy, stupid. These must be their reasons: they must have daddy issues, they must be gold diggers, they must think men are actually superior to women due to some sort of religious indoctrination, they must be doing this because they think it makes them hotter to guys. This must be who they are: uneducated, lower class, evangelical Christians, pampered suburban moms, twits.

It's really not that difficult to see why someone might choose not to be a feminist. To understand that, all we really have to do is take a look at what the feminist revolution has, and has not, offered to women.

When we all decided to be feminists, it was because we were looking at what was denied to us. We had historically been shut out of masculine spaces, like public life, the workplace, and education. Our traditional realm, of the home and the family and the nursery, looked like prisons.

What feminism thought it was offering its followers, then, was escape. It was an expanded life. A life of independence, of adventure, of work.

But in order to believe that, we have to forget that women have always worked. Many women have always had to. The unmarried, the widowed, the poor, the disadvantaged have always worked. When feminists decided to fight for the right to work, what they meant was the right to become doctors, lawyers, and so on. Women have always scrubbed toilets and floors, have always been paid to touch other people's bodies as nurses and assistants and sex workers.

Nor were women fighting to work in the jobs of poor men, the laborers and miners and slaughterhouse workers. Right from the beginning, the assumption was that work was a good thing, a fulfilling thing, that we were missing out on. Not a soul and body–destroying thing that can kill you off young or make you wish it would.

Some women have historically had an out from the realm of work. That out was through men. If they found the right man with the right situation, they could exit this soul-destroying work world and retreat to the relative comfort of the house. The house might be a prison, but when freedom looks like wiping up someone else's vomit and urine under migraine-inducing fluorescent lighting, can you actually blame someone for asking to be let back into their cell?

Poor women are not the only women who

would prefer not to work, of course. Highly educated women working in ambitious fields also
decide to check out. That "opting out" as the
feminists call it, is considered something of a betrayal. Women should work! To help their sisters
out! And yet, opting in means prioritizing long
hours at jobs over any sense of community or
family. Because in this age of precarity, work and
money are so elusive that cutting back hours can
mean a slide into irrelevance or unemployability
for many.

This is part of the problem of creating a unified
front for feminism: the median feminist is generally going to be a middle-class, educated white
woman. Her desires and needs cannot stand in
for the needs of all women. And yet we've focused on facilitating her dreams for much of re-
cent feminist history. Our goals have been things
that would make her life easier, like equal pay,
removing barriers to higher education, delaying
childbearing through birth control and fertility
treatment developments.

The workplace and capitalistic society has become increasingly hostile. Not only to women, but
to men, too. By keeping the focus on how women
are doing in the marketplace, rather than how
human beings exist under this system of competition and precarity, our thinking remains very

small. How are women faring in the job market in comparison to men? Does that really matter when due to overwhelming student loan debt, sharply decreased job stability, the gutting of social services and work benefits, rapacious CEOs and boards of directors, and globalization, the world of work and money is hurting everyone?

But sure, stick with it, sisters! We must prevail because of . . . something.

One thing we are told we must persevere for is independence. The independence of women is important. Independence from men, sure. If only because dependence on men is not what it used to be. The deal was, I give up my freedom and my body and you offer me protection from the outside world. That arrangement would last until you died.

Now of course, romance is as unstable as the job market, and just as competitive and demeaning. Unless you decide to black widow a few rich guys in a row, looking to men to provide the stability and protection you desire is unlikely to work out in a lifelong kind of way.

So it's important to have a Plan B. But why is our Plan B to manage all of it on our own? To have to, as individuals, make our money, set up our homes, bear and raise children, cook our meals, develop and maintain a sense of style and taste, decide how we spend our free time, and on and on until we die. In the name of freedom, we broke out of communities and towns and tribes and created families and blood lineage. In the name of freedom, we broke out of families and blood lineage to create a nuclear household. In the name of freedom, we broke out of nuclear households to become individuals. And yet at no point along that way did we put serious consideration into creating a social equivalent of the support system those larger groups provided to us.

True, a lot of those systems were built explicitly for the oppression of women. Community can often seem like a system for controlling behavior and insisting on conformity; family can often seem like a method of keeping women docile and tamed. But we're all so eager to overcorrect. We toss out entire systems because they once hurt us, without taking a moment to reflect on how, so often, they helped us.

Now independence is hailed as a feminist virtue. The ability to stand on one's own, outside of family or men. And now we have all the freedom and independence we desire, like the freedom to go bankrupt, to be socially isolated, to be home-

less without any social support network, to labor
all your life with nothing to show for it. As long
as feminism is still infected with the Protestant
economic determinist mindset—the idea that
your station in life is determined by how virtu-
ous you are or what you deserve—we'll continue
to put our time and energy into breaking down
social structures rather than creating new, more
empathetic ones.

And so of course a significant number of
women are going to look at this atomized, capitalistic world that feminism offers to them like
a gift and ask if they can take it back to the store
and exchange it for something a little bit more
old-fashioned. Women everywhere! Leave the
comfortable confines of traditional life and enter
this brand new world of struggle, despair, and
uncertainty! Thanks, and fuck you, but no.

Not every woman, or man, is ambitious. Not
every woman is determined to make her mark
on the world. Not every woman gets satisfaction
out of working eighty hours a week just to watch
some young Harvard asshole get promoted above
her to a job she didn't really want but would pay
her a little better. Not every woman longs to participate in the consumerist mindfuck that is the
culture we live in, filling the holes in her heart
and soul with shoes and limited edition crop tops

from Topshop. It's feminism's fault that these are
the two options we have available to women. Either you can let a man take care of the financial
and outer world side of things while you spend
time with your children and shop for overpriced
organic blueberries, or you can work until you
die to buy stuff you don't need and fight for every
square inch you exist on. Either that pays off for
you in the end or it doesn't.

When—let's call them "traditional"—women
"feel sorry" for feminists, they're doing pretty
much what we do to them. We are using pity as a
self-defense mechanism. We feel sorry for someone so we don't have to assign value to anything
they say or do or believe. We do not have to listen
to their complaints about our beliefs.

And yet if we were able to sit down, without
judgment, and ask what we're not offering these
women, we might actually be able to get somewhere. Not along the lines of conversion. We
need to stop thinking that way. Instead, we could
see the limitations of our own project; that we're
not as smart as we think we are; that maybe the
ways these women are unhappy line up with the
ways we are unhappy.

If you look at what is missing from today's society, much of it falls within traditional feminine values and pursuits. Carving out space within the masculine realm, in the work and public spheres, meant in part abandoning the feminine spheres of home, care, and community. There was no equal effort to make space for men in the feminine pursuits. As a result, what you see is a kind of hyper-masculinized world, where women are participating—and absolutely expected to participate in this world by feminists—in patriarchal values.

Feminism has been marred by these patriarchal values. It has been warped in the name of greed and power. Feminism was seduced by all the pleasures the patriarchal world has to offer and overwhelmed by the enormous amount of work it would take to break it apart. So we adapted feminism's goals in order to live more comfortable lives.

In order to succeed in a patriarchal world, we took on the role of patriarchs ourselves. In order to win in this world, we had to exhibit the characteristics the patriarchal world values and discard what it does not.

In order to get ahead in this culture, we also shape ourselves to what men value in women, which is sexuality and beauty. Never before has there been such pressure to maintain our sexual availability throughout our lives, and women celebrities who keep their figures, who are still hot after all these years, are praised as role models by feminists.

We've been cut off from traditions and rituals, from family and intergenerational connections, from communities and a sense of belonging. We saw these things as unpaid labor that we were forced to do, rather than something worth preserving. It is true that we were forced into these roles, but it's also true that these things have value and should be maintained. It goes beyond squabbling over who does the housework and childcare in a nuclear family, to the question of how do we feel like we belong somewhere? How do we begin to value giving as much as we value taking? How do we participate in and contribute to the world, outside of the jobs we have? How do we think of our place in society, beyond being an individual or being part of a couple or nuclear family? These will be the challenges of feminism moving forward.

Our job, as feminists, should not be recruitment. It should not be conversion. It should be listening to the wants and needs of women that might differ from our own. The condescending attitude of Western feminists toward women in Muslim countries—this idea that these women need to be rescued from their head scarves and their traditions—is a good illustration of that. Never mind the fact that rescue and protection are masculine, patriarchal ideas. Our attempts at conversion are asking women to devalue what they find valuable about their existence, to take on our values of independence, success, and sexuality.

And yet despite our attempts at converting women to our values, we rarely seem to pause and ask ourselves if these things actually make us happy. If this way of life is the best we can do. To question this is not to run screaming back to the kitchen, to allow men to make our decisions for us and go back to our subjugation. It is to ask if maybe there were things we discarded that we should go back and reclaim. It's to ask if maybe we need to pause for a moment and rethink not only our strategy but also our goals.

There are questions we need to ask ourselves. They're going to make us uncomfortable. The first: Has feminism created a better world? Not just for you personally, but for both women and men in all levels of society. The next: Has feminism created the space for men to take on traditionally feminine traits at the same level it has created the space for women to take on traditionally masculine traits? And lastly: If we say we want a better world for women, are the current goals and ideas of feminism likely to create that world?

3

Every Option
Is Equally Feminist

It's no surprise that Andrea Dworkin has become the go-to scapegoat for younger feminists, the physical and intellectual embodiment of those moments when feminism "went too far." In contrast to the blogs and books that reassure readers that feminism can be "sexy," here stands Andrea Dworkin, obese, frizzy-haired, without even a hint of lipgloss.

She is a terror for women afraid of going too far, afraid that if they acknowledge the unfair and ridiculous standards for their behavior, appearance, and conduct, they will actually come to reject those standards, and from there it's a slippery slope to tossing out your hair products and your $30 blush and your contouring brushes and your $400 high heels, the ones that you can't even walk in but have to pack in your bag for changing into in the taxi on the way to the event, lest you break both your ankles just going up a few steps. Suddenly you'll find yourself in sweatpants, talking to strangers in the grocery store or just on the sidewalk about how you don't even actually have to wash your hair, your hair is self-cleansing and really so much healthier once you stop shampooing it, just a little baking soda, that's all you need. This is the fear that haunts all the feminists trying to reject their radical predecessors: that if we understand the mechanism of control, if we see through the bullshit that keeps us anxious, keeps us worried about our dress size and our stylish presentation, if we understand that we are wasting our lives in jobs that are contributing to the evil of the world and oppressing the poor, then we are actually going to have to do something about it, god damn it. And that just sounds uncomfortable.

Discomfort is not part of the universal feminist agenda. It can't be, if it wants to appeal to all women. Universal feminists want a feminism that does not require changing the way you dress, think, or behave. With all the focus now on opinion and personal narratives (over theory or even fact), it tells young feminists that they do not have to study their own collective and intellectual history. With all of the focus on lifestyle, contemporary feminism becomes just another thing to buy.

Of course the universal feminists want to remove Dworkin from the face of feminism, along with every other woman who resembles her. Just from her appearance alone, Dworkin makes an easy target, something to gesture toward to illustrate just how harmless you are in comparison. And in her place, Gloria Steinem—that banal, CIA-funded icon for white, middle-class women—becomes the only feminist from the last half of the twentieth century worth knowing about. It's not just Dworkin's appearance that makes women uncomfortable. It's her writing, which was merciless. Like all writers and intellectuals, not every word Dworkin wrote was magic, but the entirety of her work seems to have been tossed out by today's feminists, simply because they disagree with some of her more extreme theories. Michel Foucault believed AIDS didn't actually exist and was merely a social construct, but that doesn't mean we refuse to read anything else he wrote, or that we use him as an example of when gays "went too far."

What makes feminists uncomfortable about Dworkin (and MacKinnon and Kate Millett and Valerie Solanas and others) was that she demanded that women think hard about what it was they were participating in. That's it. By participating, you are in a way condoning that institution, that activity, that way of life. Not only condoning, but propping up. Dworkin demanded that women contemplate their interpersonal relationships, their work, their everyday existence out in the world, to see how it requires participation in systems of oppression and misery. All of the excuses we make for why we cannot possibly change our lives, why we cannot become radicals ("I have student loans, so I need this job," ". . . but I love him," "I have dreamed about owning a house and becoming a mother and getting married since I was a little girl and it would really be disappointing if suddenly I had to understand what property ownership really is etc., etc.") brought before Dworkin's point of view are instantly rendered bullshit.

The most infamous example of this is her book *Intercourse*, which examined the power dynamics in male-female sexual relationships: the male-oriented emphasis on penetration as the default sex act, the way personal desire is shaped by culture, and how tricky issues of consent are in an imbalanced society. People saw this complicated (and wildly relevant to today's conversation about "rape culture") work and summed up its position as, "All sex is rape." Women participated in this slander, because the book asked them to do something difficult that they did not want to do: Look at what you are participating in when you are engaged sexually or romantically with a male partner. Think about the power dynamic. Think about your own autonomy, think about how you are contributing to these imbalances through your personal choices. Who wants to do that? Easier, then, to dismiss the book as nonsense so that you don't have to listen to its message. Easier to swallow something like *The Feminine Mystique* and other more mainstream work that claimed women were the victims of some external structure or institution, rather than active participants in their own subjugation. Easier to think we are rendered absolutely powerless than to think we choose powerlessness because it is more convenient.

There was no and is no generosity in the response to radical feminist work, either by women or by men. This campaign to erase the radicals from feminist history is regrettable. Rather than reading them within their context, empathizing with their position, allowing enough vulnerability to start to see your own life through their lens, we are to toss them out as jokes. Dworkin and her kin cannot be prettied up and made palatable.

And so you see this online:

A man says feminism is a bunch of man-haters. "What about that Dworkin bitch who said all men are rapists?"

Feminist women ring in, reassuring him. "We don't like her either."

That refusal to experience the discomfort of real change, and this rejection of the radical feminist position, has led to what is called "choice feminism." This is the belief that no matter what a woman chooses, from her lifestyle to her family dynamic to her pop culture consumption, she is making a feminist choice, just from the act of choosing anything. The idea is that under the more rigidly patriarchal past, women's choices were made for them. So simply by choosing anything at all, you are bucking the patriarchy and acting like a feminist.

This is what universal feminism, devoid of any real personal internal change, leads to. In the same way that any woman can become a feminist simply by declaring herself a feminist, any act can become a feminist act simply by a woman insisting it's a feminist act. No debate, no consideration, no discomfort required.

We all secretly know where we are fucking

up, where we are not doing enough, where we are letting ourselves and the rest of the world down. We expend a shit-ton of physical, emotional, and mental energy ignoring that knowledge and pretending it's not there, so we lash out at those who remind us of our deficiencies.

We know—god, WE KNOW, shut up already—that that cute top was sewn by children, in a factory with such lax safety standards that at almost any moment the whole thing could go, taking hundreds of lives with it. But fuck it, we want that top. We know—WE KNOW—that if we buy this cheap grocery store rotisserie chicken that this animal knew only suffering for the entirety of its life, and that the farmer who raised it is kept impoverished and in crushing debt by the massive food corporations they are contracted to. But fuck it, the organic chicken is $7 more and not even cooked yet and it was a long day at the office. And hey, we also know that the corporations we work for poison the earth, fleece the poor, make the super rich even more rich, but hey. Fuck it. We like our apartments, we can subscribe to both Netflix and Hulu, the health insurance covers my SSRI prescription, and the white noise machine I just bought helps me sleep at night.

And anyway, where to begin? How can any-

one ever deal with the overwhelming despair of
the world without being subsumed by it?

One way we deal with the cognitive dissonance is to attack the true radicals. They awaken
that secret knowledge in us; to quiet it back
down, we must destroy them. Call them hu-
morless hags, call them wackos. Refuse to read
their work but offer public criticisms of it anyway. And then, of course, investigate their lives
for imperfections and hypocrisies and—instead
of recognizing that everyone is human, everyone
has flaws—use those imperfections to discredit a
lifetime of work. Anything to give you the excuse
not to listen and not to change.

A true radical response is a lonely road, but
it's super hip these days to think of yourself as a
radical without doing anything to deserve it. To
think that if you buy this special bag of tortilla
chips with a pink ribbon on it, you are helping to
cure cancer. That if you buy this album and wear
a leather jacket, you are a true punk. And if you
simply call yourself a feminist, you are a feminist.

Suddenly those choices you've made aren't so
fraught after all, because you're cloaking them in
a thin veil of feminism. The cognitive dissonance
disappears. That top? A personal expression of
your true self. Wearing that top is a display of
your individuality, totally feminist. That chicken?

You are *nurturing* yourself, you're nourishing your body. Totally feminist because it's body-positive. And your job? You are climbing the ladder of success, you are shattering glass ceilings for the women who come after you, you are self-empowered and asking for a raise that you totally deserve. That is probably the most feminist thing of all.

Choice feminism is a major problem with white feminism. We take our experiences of being thwarted, of being discriminated against and put down, our encounters with violence and pain, and we use these experiences to justify taking what we want, without ever examining why we want it.

Much of white feminism was built on the idea of "consciousness-raising" sessions where women were given space to think about and vocalize times in their lives when they faced misogyny and conflict, maybe in a way they didn't recognize at the time. That light bulb goes off when we realize that teacher who discouraged us did it because I was a girl pursuing a "boy" subject, not because I didn't possess potential. Issues that women had formerly thought of as personal could then be seen as universal, or at least shared with larger parts of the population.

But consciousness raising stalls out when people do not use the same methods to examine the future as well as the past. How do you create a future that is better for everyone and not just yourself? How do we fight for the good of all of humanity, not just this particular segment of women, the women who resemble us?

I say "white feminism" because many of the goals of mainstream feminism benefit middle-class white women, and also because those are the women who became, and remain, the most visible representatives of the movement. We talk about the second wave as fighting for economic equality, but in the lower realms of income, where minority women were dwelling in larger numbers, that inequality endured. The radical part of the second wave we tend to forget was even part of the movement.

Many of the ideas that were floated as potential goals for second wave feminism never found traction with the movement at large, because once you reached a certain level of money or fame, it would be more personally advantageous for you to fight for your own needs rather than contribute to a system that offered fairness for all. Take childcare for example, an issue that never gets much support beyond lip service in the feminist world, despite it being something that would benefit the majority of women. Once you reach a certain income level, it's easier and more convenient for you to take care of your own childcare needs than to pay the taxes or contribute to a system that would help all women. If your child is in a failing school, it's much more convenient to place your child in a private or charter school than to organize ways to improve the situation for the entire community. This also applies to expanding social welfare programs, supporting community clinics, and so on. As a woman's ability to take care of herself expands thanks to feminist efforts, the feminist goals she's willing to really fight for, or contribute time and money and effort to, shrink. The women who did not benefit in the same way are not really her problem, which is why mainstream feminists now just fight for the right to make their own decisions, no matter what they are.

These consciousness-raising sessions gave us the idea that the personal is political. But that is a phrase that has been misinterpreted for years. For a very long time, women have been taking this to mean that their own personal victories are political victories. If I claw my way to the top of a big Hollywood studio, then I don't really have to do anything to make the place more friendly to women, I don't have to stand my ground to give more room for women's voices. Just my being here is a political win. Whatever the other uses of the phrase, the one that we seem to have overlooked most frequently is the idea that personal decisions have political ramifications and that those ramifications should be examined and taken into consideration. Choice feminism blocks any discussion about these issues, about the consequences of how people choose to live their lives. Because the choice itself is feminist, any criticism one might have is invalid. It's her personal choice, it's her journey. With this mindset, criticizing a feminist is a form of oppression.

This sets up a false us-versus-them mentality. There's us, the poor, hindered, victimized women, and then there are the men who are trying to keep us down. Except that most obstacles for women have been removed by now. Women are allowed to go to college, to work in traditionally masculine fields, to speak in public, to run for office, to do whatever they want. The actual obstacles and inequalities that women face are mostly obstacles only for the poor—middle-class women and above can now buy their access to power and equality. The issues most pressing for lower income women, like affordable abortions, childcare, health insurance and health care, public housing, and so on, have slipped off the feminist radar. We may have opinions about these things, but the actual work of improving them is lacking.

It's not us versus them, it's every woman for herself. What there really should be is a discussion about how women less advantaged than us (or living in different countries or different cultures) are oppressed by the things we think of as empowering. Yet there is real resistance to this discussion, particularly online and on college campuses. Lately, older feminist writers and activists have been vilified by the younger generation for not using the right language, for arguing points that are no longer fashionable, and for just taking a different point of view.

This is the way dissent is handled in feminist realms: a contrary opinion or argument is actually an attack. This stems from the belief that your truth is the only truth, that your sense of trauma and oppression does not need to be examined or questioned.

In this environment, it's impossible to have actual, productive conversations about the way your choices affect other people.

•   •   •

Feminism is—should be—a movement, not an excuse to stand still. But when the only authority you need to answer to is yourself, you create a feedback loop of logic. Everything is justifiable, everything somehow rendered feminist.

And yet what is the point of having principles or a philosophical viewpoint if you don't use them to live your life by, to move yourself and your society forward? Dworkin did not take things too far. We didn't take things far enough.

4

How Feminism Ended Up
Doing Patriarchy's Work

There is a way a woman can deflect the worst effects of patriarchal control, and that is through money. Make enough of it and you can escape the patriarchy's most obvious trappings. You will be listened to, you will be allowed a space in public life, and you can avoid being forced into a care position like so many other women—you can pay someone else to do that for you. To cook your food, to launder your clothing, to tend to your children. Money is a quick and easy way to check out of many pernicious forms of oppression. And women have more and more of it.

That's what many of us have decided to do: buy our way out of the patriarchy. Most of the ways women are kept under control can be thwarted financially, from paying for medical services many women cannot afford to circumventing legal inequalities with hired lawyers and respectability.

Every institution in my native country, the United States, from the justice system to the banking industry, from real estate to the educational system, is a product of, and a means of support to, the patriarchy. Marriage is a patriarchal support. Consumer culture is a patriarchal support.

Our educational system exploits its teachers and adjuncts, privileges the moneyed. How much money you have determines the quality of education you receive, and it often drives the non-moneyed further into poverty by saddling them with tens of thousands of dollars of debt. This is a form of patriarchal control. In marriage, men benefit from higher salaries and better health while women still carry the burden of lowered income, longer hours of housework, and child care. This is a form of patriarchal control.

The patriarchy is more than a matter of a woman's personal freedom. It is not us versus them. It is the system by which the powerful maintain their position through the control and the oppression of the many. Misogyny, as well as racism, homophobia, and whatever word we will come up with to classify the pretty obvious fear and hatred of the impoverished that dominates

our public life, is a logical outgrowth of the patriarchy. In order to take advantage of someone,
in order to think of them as a resource to be ex-
ploited, it helps to dehumanize them.

It follows that women who are a part of the
system are not necessarily any better, morally
speaking, than the men who developed and
maintained it. Women are now lawyers and
judges who put innocent men and women in jail,
who exploit the poor, who support institutional-
ized racism. Women are now politicians who are
rewarding the mega-rich with even more money
at the expense of the poor.

When an industry has gone off the rails, like
Wall Street or Silicon Valley, you hear this a lot:
"They just need more women. Women have more
common sense, more empathy. It's just a boys
club run wild." This is illogical. It's humans, not
men, who are the problem here.

Now that women are raised with access to
power, we will not see a more egalitarian world,
but the same world, just with more women in it.

The feminist and civil rights movements shared
a common goal: to dismantle the hierarchy by
which Western society had been organized for

centuries. At the top rested the landowning and
moneyed white men. Beneath them was everyone
else, although the order of the lower levels shifted
through the ages. But these movements destroyed
the hierarchy, putting everyone on a theoretically
level playing field. It's obviously still an incom-
plete job, but with every generation of white boys
who are not raised to believe they have dominion
over everyone else, and every generation of everyone else who is not raised to believe they must
be subservient, these identifying markers of race
and sex will no longer guarantee your place in
society.

Why, then, are women still operating within
systems of power? Because we have replaced gender and race with money and power. Now you
can buy your position in society rather than have
to be born with the right genetics. Now that we
have access as women, women in positions of
power are much less likely to attempt to dismantle this system of inequality. Power feels good.
Capitalism feels good. It gives you things, as long
as its boot is not on your neck.

Certainly, there have been many men throughout time who understood that the hierarchy of
gender and race was inherently immoral and un-
just. But white men were never going to rise up
en masse to destroy it and grant liberty and equal

rights to all. It suited them too well. Even if they did not have power themselves, they had at least the possibility of gaining it in the future. Power is blinding.

This is also why universal feminism will always be toothless. Because a feminism that springs from self-interest, that is embraced because it more easily gives access to power—rather than being embraced out of any social awareness—will necessarily be part of this system of power and oppression, and so meaningless as a way toward universal human rights. Women are now active participants in this system and they are benefiting from it.

Gone are the days when all women were united behind a single cause. Your ability to break away from subjugation is different from mine, and that is due to differences in race, attractiveness, personal history, class, location, education, occupation, and so on. To insist that all women's experiences or desires are the same is folly: they simply are not.

When women as a whole were discriminated against due to biological facts, and that discrimination was written directly into the law books, it made sense to claim solidarity. There were universal needs and universal obstacles that could bind us together.

But today my subjugation will look different from yours. The obstacles I face are different than the obstacles you face, because most of the universal obstacles have been removed. We also have to accept that some of the obstacles that we call misogyny are not actually discrimination against women. We are women, but it might be more helpful to think of ourselves as humans first.

This brings into question why we still need feminism. To finish the job of destroying the hierarchy, sure. There are issues of reproductive rights, sexual violence, and so on, that are still active barriers to women's freedom. We should not become complacent and stop fighting. Our lives and the lives of the generation to come will still require struggle.

But if we are moving toward parity—and all educational, entrepreneurial, economic, and public office holding rates, when we look at the median woman's advance, suggest that we are— does it make sense to base our ideology around our biological identities? With our needs, our desires, our obstacles, and our circumstances so diverse, what unifies us? We also have to consider what we lose by insisting women are distinctly different from men, how that myth both serves us and hurts us.

Here is one way feminism is still a useful idea: Almost all of us have been marginalized in one way or another due to our gender. That marginalization should allow us to see that it's the whole system that is corrupt. Being marginalized should give women the perspective and power to see the system's workings and its dark heart.

This version of feminism, which could do much to change society as a whole, is at a powerful moment, because we have people on the inside as well as the outside. We are at the city's walls, but we have also infiltrated the center. If we were able to align ourselves and see that the whole thing needed to come down—this society based on greed, this society that is killing so many through poverty, violence, and exploitation—we could do it.

Unfortunately, many will think the only thing wrong with the system—and by "system" I mean this whole complicated world that we inadequately convey with words like "patriarchy" or "capitalism"—is that it is not allowing them entry. The whole thing is rigged to include some and exclude others, to benefit some and exploit others, therefore it is evil. By fighting for your own way to inclusion, you are not improving the system, you are simply joining the ranks of those included and benefiting. You are doing your own excluding and exploiting. In other words: you, a woman, are also the patriarchy.

If we accept our marginalization, we can take a moment to think about what kind of world we would be participating in if we were granted inclusion. Because once women are fully accepted—and this day is coming—once we wield power instead of having power wielded against us, there will be no time to pause and reflect. Simply put, once we are a part of the system and benefiting from it on the same level that men are, we won't care, as a group, about whose turn it is to get hurt. But we carry obligations toward everyone we share space with, just by virtue of sharing space with them. And those obligations come before any of our own so-called rights or entitlements.

We keep losing women to participation in the system, instead of insubordination to the system. The idea that you can make the strongest impact by influencing the culture from the inside is naive at best, disingenuous at worst.

It is one thing, for example, to go to law school

for the explicit purpose of devoting your life to protecting the vulnerable from the system. That is insubordination. That devotion requires a radicalization process that is rarely encouraged in feminist culture these days. To be radicalized, you often have to be mentored through the process, and there are few active radical feminists today who are listened to and who are included in the current conversation.

This idea that women will "change the culture" of any given industry is an easy lie to buy into. Even if women go in with good intentions, good intentions are nothing against the system. The system is older than you. It has absorbed more venom than you can ever hope to emit. You will not even slow it down.

In order to gain entry, you will have to exhibit the characteristics of the patriarchs who built it. In order to advance, you will have to mimic their behavior, take on their values. Their values are power, the love of power, and the display of power. By then, you are part of their culture.

Few will want to admit their real reasons for buying into the system. It's nice in there. It feels good. You get things. If you say things people want to hear, people will listen to you. Attention feels good. If you value power, people will give you power, and with that comes money, luxury, a way out of all of that oppression and misery. Little thought will be given to those left on the outside.

Once you get to that place, you are not so much a sell-out as a buyer-in.

And trust me: people will hate you if you choose freedom over money, if you decide to live a life by your values of compassion, honesty, and integrity. Because you will remind them of their own deficiencies in these areas.

It's lonely outside the system. But we need you out here.

The other power our marginalization could give us is the ability to align and empathize with the others who are also on the outs. All those labeled worthless by those in charge, from people of color to religious minorities to the poor. There could be an alliance there.

The fact that there is not only not an alliance, but that feminism has been guilty throughout its history of rampant racism, homophobia, xeno-phobia, and other failures of empathy, shows that the mainstream goal was always participation in the system, rather than its destruction. The goal was to share in the power, not to reveal this powerful/powerless dynamic as evil. The only thing that made the system evil in our eyes was that we were not granted access. We saw, and still see, the other marginalized not as our equals, but as competition for power once the hierarchy falls.

Being marginalized should have awoken us to how the system works. It should have made us acutely aware of the other vulnerable populations, the other people who were not protected. Instead it made us selfish. It made us focused on our own advancement, our own entitlement. Fighting for your own self-interest, without the awareness of your motives or the ramifications of your success, does not make you a hero. It makes you the same as any other selfish, ambitious jerk.

Right now, women are in a unique position. We are halfway in. We are on both sides of the powerful/powerless dynamic. It should be easy, then, to rip the fucker apart by pulling on both sides.

You will not find eager volunteers, though, among those on power's side, for obvious reasons. Neither on the powerless side. The position of the powerless is often a state of being primed for acquisition. As long as there is a glimmer of a chance that they can switch sides, even if that glimmer is a complete illusion, people will fight to keep the system that oppresses them in place. Just in case they are finally given the opportunity to oppress someone else for a change.

5

Self-Empowerment
Is Just Another Word
for *Narcissism*

In order to withstand the pressure of a culture constantly telling us that women are only meat, only sex, only property, we create this idea of our specialness. We as women are naturally more compassionate, more loving, more authentic than men. This idea shores us up against the constant degradation caused simply by living in this particular time and place.

Sometimes we as women are special in our compassion. For people to be able to survive on the margins, they often must be. They must form alliances, they must look out for one another. They must develop some characteristics and attributes because they have to create networks of solidarity and mutual care to withstand the experience of marginalization. Those characteristics are developed by facing hardship and opposition.

We also have to find ways of convincing our op-
pressors not to hurt us, not to kill us, to bother
keeping us around at all. That can make us clever.

But these attributes are not innate. In fact, the
idea that women are naturally more empathetic
and nurturing originates with men. They used it
as an excuse to keep us at home, tending to the
children. They used it as an excuse to dismiss us
intellectually. Don't try to be smart, sweetheart,
it's not your strong suit. And yet we adopted this
belief because it suits us to believe it about ourselves. It makes us special.

What should make us feel special instead is
our method of survival. If we believe these skills
are born into us we will lose them once they are
no longer needed. We can still use the lie as a
cover, as a way to avoid questioning or reckoning.
"Oh, I'm a woman, so of course I'm going to be
a better listener, more emotionally attuned, I am
definitely not going to abandon these principles
and work in my own self interest given the first
opportunity, just like everyone else."

Currently, I see this as women line up behind
female politicians, their support thrown behind
them almost solely because they share a gender.
Despite a long history of supporting military in-
tervention, I watch women talk about these politicians' natural diplomacy and how they'll keep

us out of war. Despite a long history of gutting social services, I watch women talk about these politicians' understanding and attention to poor women and children. Despite a long history of money grabbing and corruption, I watch women talk about these politicians' sense of fairness and economic justice. If the genders were reversed, that support would be withdrawn. There would be no assumption that these politicians would act more ethically and compassionately than their male counterparts unless these women had convinced themselves that these qualities are inherent in all women.

We tell ourselves this story to withstand our culture, yes. But certain stories stop being helpful. They change from being tools to being weapons. The idea that women are naturally kinder is a tool that has morphed in just this way.

Our belief in innate gender qualities comes through clearly with the language we use to discuss the situations of both men and women. We use terms like "toxic masculinity," we refer unquestioningly to the "problems" testosterone creates in a way we would become outraged by if men referred to the "problems" estrogen creates. These are all ways of distancing ourselves from human qualities we want to deny in ourselves. No one talks about toxic femininity, but certainly if we look at certain feminine modes in contemporary culture, it exists. But we would prefer to think of toxic masculinity as innate, and any problems with women's behavior as being socially created. It's convenient.

Saying or believing that women are special also, by default, dehumanizes men. If we are special because we are caring, then men must be uncaring. If we are special because we are compassionate and nurturing, then men must be emotionally dead and destructive. And if these qualities are innate, then we can dismiss the entire male gender. And in doing so, we are being merely descriptive, not judgmental.

The easiest way to feel empowered is to claim identification with some sort of group (gender, nationality, religion, etc). It is the laudable characteristics of that group that you identify as your own characteristics, which are based on the way a gender, a nation, or a religion prefers to think about itself.

The easiest way for a group to build its sense of

identity is through the rejection or the demeaning of that group's "opposite." In order for atheists to present themselves as rational and intelligent, they have to present the religious as superstitious and foolish. This is certainly easier and more effective than consistently being rational and intelligent. In order for America to think of itself as strong and important, it has to think of Europe as being weak and worthless. And in order for women to think of themselves as compassionate, they have to think of men as violent.

Part of this is simple projection. All the aspects of yourself that you are ashamed of or fear that you possess (weakness, anger, irrationality) can be easily forgotten if you assign those traits to someone you are not. If you strongly identify as one thing, your opposite can be not only a scapegoat, but a shit storehouse. Anything you'd like to distance yourself from can simply be stored in the identity of your opposite. "This group over here is _____ [enter whatever disgusting thing you can't bear to see inside of yourself]. I belong to the group that is the opposite of this, and so therefore I possess the opposite qualities."

This is meant to convince both yourself and your audience of your value. When someone has a gap in their sense of self, or in their sense of the value of themselves, that gap can be filled with the sense of the group with which they identify. Nationalism tends to strengthen during times of struggle. Individuals fall on hard times, they find themselves suffering from unemployment or poverty or displacement, which causes self-doubt. People erase that self-doubt, or at least cover it up, by suddenly proclaiming participation in a larger project, the project of a nation. Their nation is great, their nation has a tremendous history, and so they are allowed to participate in that greatness, to possess it, to play a part in that tremendous history.

Nationalism, in and of itself, is not bad. Identifying with a larger group is not, in and of itself, bad. Particularly when a group has been degraded and dismissed. The act of coming together, of saying, "These things that you dismiss as worthless, they have value," is a meaningful act.

And so it has been for much of feminist history: the act of reclaiming the work and characteristics of femininity that have been dismissed as worthless by the patriarchal system. From the care work of raising children and keeping homes, to the traditional crafts of quilting and knitting, to the stories of fairy tales and folk wisdom. These "feminine" things are valuable, and it is important for them to be considered valuable by both men and women. Men should be invited to participate in these traditions, but in order for that to happen we must remember not to mistake what is "feminine" with what is "female."

Reclamation is hard work. Finding the value in your group's characteristics means always having to confront the darkness in those characteristics. For example, it is acceptable, and productive, to think of America as a great nation. It has many great characteristics, from the freedom it grants its citizens to the cultural contributions it has fostered and rewarded. But by unearthing America's good qualities, you will also find its destructive qualities. The way it has interfered internationally and created death and misery for countless citizens of other nations, its history of genocide and slavery, and so on. It is possible to know America's destructive power and still think it is a great nation. But some prefer not to look at all, so as to avoid the cognitive dissonance.

It is always easier to find your sense of value by demeaning another's value. It is easier to define yourself as "not that," than to do an actual accounting of your own qualities.

Which is why the casual hatred of men as a gender is so disturbing. It is the same thing men have done to women for centuries. In order not to feel weak, they projected weakness onto us. In order not to feel emotional, they projected their emotions onto us. Now when women want not to feel foolish, they project foolishness onto men. When they want not to feel destructive, they project their destructiveness onto men.

Through this act of projection, we are not only refusing to see the full humanity of men, we are refusing to see the full humanity of ourselves. We are not fully human if we only accept our good bits. There is not much variety if we only use the light colors of the spectrum.

And so, according to a brief perusal of women writer's comments online over the past few days, men are: overly confident, predatory, helpless, psychopaths, terrified of women, fascists, the reason why the world is in this mess, literally so stupid, and the problem here.

Of course what these women really mean is that they themselves are not overly confident, not predatory, not helpless, and on down the line. It's just easier to say that men are these things, than that you are not these things. People would rightly become suspicious if you suddenly started going on about how amazing you were. They'd start looking for proof you weren't. But by attributing these negative behaviors and traits to your "opposite" group, it's an easy, criticism-proof way of saying, "I would never behave like this, I would never be like this."

And look, it's funny, and it probably even feels like a public service, deflating the male ego. They think too much of themselves, obviously, or they wouldn't think they and they alone could run the world for so long. This is just bringing men's view of themselves into better alignment with who they actually are. And yet it seems to me if we really were better than them, we wouldn't simply pick up all of their bad habits. We could find some value in ourselves without demeaning the value of men.

It is also worth examining the effect such projection has on each respective group—both the projector and the projected upon. Defining a group by their negative characteristics in order to define yourself as "at least not that" has a way of hardening that exact unwanted characteristic.

When the Serbs wanted to demonize the Bosnians, one way was to emphasize their Muslim identity. Before the war, Bosnian Muslims were mostly secular in attitude and dress. After the war, there was an increase in veiling women and religious observance. It's an act of defiance, a way of reclaiming what has been dismissed or, in this case, demonized. Traditions that had been falling out of fashion were suddenly deemed important: This is why they hated us. Best to celebrate what they hate.

As for the group doing the projecting, once you start projecting, it excuses you from examining your own ability to do harm. If they're the bad guys, then you're the good guys, and so anything you do against them is for the greater good. It's why anyone who disagrees with you in political discourse is immediately Hitler. It doesn't matter what you do or say against Hitler. Just by him or her being Hitler, you are immediately the good soul. Even if your methods to bring this person down are dirty, this person is Hitler. The ends justify the means, and the ends are justified by this projection.

Whenever we feel superior to anyone else, we take away that person's humanity in order to bolster our own sense of self and worth. We take directly from them what we need to compensate for our own lack. We see their confidence, their certainty, as surplus. We need it, and so we find reasons to take it.

Once an oppressor's power starts to slip, it is very easy to switch places and adopt the same behavior. In order to oppress us, they had to dehumanize us. And we dehumanized them back, while we were at their mercy. After all, only monsters could treat human beings so. This is easier than trying to understand the way a human becomes an oppressor, the process by which anyone, including our own special selves, can find ourselves in that role. When the power changes hands, as it always eventually does, it is easy to continue to think of these humans as monsters, as we dole out punishment or revenge. If they are monsters, it doesn't matter what we say or do to them, or think about them. In our minds, they are the oppressor, we are the victims.

It is a dangerous thing to combine a victim mentality with a dehumanizing outlook. Now we become the persecutor, but backed up with our absolute certainty that we are the persecuted, we are the dehumanized, we are the victims. This victim mentality becomes a shield, so we do not have to examine what it is we are doing. It's for our protection, obviously. Much in the same way our "monsters" took up this view of us—that we were somehow less than human—so that they would not have to think about what they were doing to us.

There is also the allure of revenge here. Any group that has been oppressed for any length of time feeds itself on revenge fantasies, which we see playing out in the mob justice of social media.

It's a natural state that results from the conditions under which women have been placed. We may deny these feelings, but evidence of them is clear. It's not enough to feel victorious. Someone else has to lose. Almost every fight for freedom goes off the rails in this way: the Irish began bombing civilians, protestors in Tahrir Square began abusing and raping women, Colombian guerillas attacked the impoverished farmers on whose behalf they swore to be working.

But we'll say this time it will be different. After all, we're women. This is a toxic masculinity problem. We don't have to think about our rage or our capacity for violence because those are the problems of men.

And yet women have participated in almost every fight for freedom. They were there when civilians were targeted, they were there when bombs were planted. To argue they didn't have enough power to speak up or they had been brainwashed by their male colleagues is to try to disassociate from the darkness that resides in everyone. And to disassociate from your darkness is to lose your power over it.

•   •   •

There is a tendency toward using suffering as a reason to withhold compassion and care. We have suffered, we have faced oppression, and so now we deserve to be selfish. We deserve to focus on bettering our own situation, because we have been through so much.

In the industry in which I work, publishing, the majority of the workers are white women. More women work in publishing than men. They are executives, editors, publicists, interns. Women also populate literary prize committees, literary magazines, bookstores, book sections of newspapers. While the very top positions are disproportionately held by men, the mass of the industry is run by female labor.

There have been major inroads, then, over the past several years, in publishing and supporting books by women. Ratios of women authors published have increased, the number of women winning literary awards and being awarded grants and fellowships have increased. There is a serious, well-documented conversation in the literary world about sexism and access for women, and real action has been taken to address imbalances on almost every level.

By "women," above, I of course mean "white women." I of course mean middle to upper-class, well-educated white women.

Less noticeable, less dominant, is the conversation about the access of writers of color to the literary power center. Below that is the access of LGBTQ, of the disabled, of the economically disadvantaged.

In other words, a certain class of women were able to access literature's power center. There they made changes to facilitate their peers' migration into the power center. There, women defend their power against interlopers, like writers of color or writers who come from poverty. They fight for their own self-interest or for the interest of those who very closely resemble themselves, and use the inequalities they faced as justification for their actions.

(One should notice that the women who were granted access very closely resemble the men who used to exclusively hold power: by class, by race, by educational system, by physical location. They very often share the same views and values. In a way, this is not a victory for inclusion so much as a slight redefinition of the terms of exclusion.)

With women taking up more than half of the publishing jobs, one would think they would create an open environment, one where all groups were granted equal access. And yet that has not happened. When questions have been raised about why publishing remains such an exclusive venture, weak gestures have been made in the direction of the "patriarchy" as an explanation. Yet, despite gaining power, women have kept the conversation focused on their lack of power.

It's easier to complain about the power you don't have than to think about how you are wielding the power you do have. Simply re-creating the exclusive systems and inequities that the industry had when it was male dominated—with the only difference being that a small subsection of women are inside rather than outside—has not made the industry fairer. And because they are able to blame the creators of the system, their own actions can go unquestioned, despite their efforts to retain that exclusivity and unfairness.

Women, because they are humans, work and operate as humans, which is to say, in a clannish mode. But with the added emphasis on identity in today's society, with identifying yourself as a woman first and a human second, this clannishness becomes entrenched. Solidarity becomes not about all womankind, but about the women in proximity to you, the women you can see yourself in.

•   •   •

It is natural to want to benefit from your struggle. You suffered through scarcity and lack, discrimination and humiliation. You came through to the other side to finally create a space of your own. And now you want that to pay off. That's why it's easier to keep the focus on our powerlessness, to blame someone else for the unfairness of it all. That way, we can still benefit from our new positions without being asked to account for them in the way that men currently are.

We watched for decades, centuries, as men benefited from their positions. We learned how they closed off entryways, how they subtly manipulated us into believing we wouldn't even like this stuff. It's boring, really, you wouldn't like it. Such a chore. And we saw how they benefited, not just financially, but emotionally, from their positions. Of course we want the same thing. And they are our model, the patriarchal way of doing things is the only way we have seen things done.

A major way men of letters kept women of letters in a subordinate position was to value men's writing. They valued the characteristics displayed in male writing, insisted it was the best, and, for the most part, forced women to either give up on the possibility of institutional respect and acceptance or to mimic their ways. They insisted taste is objective. They did not question what their taste said about them and their politics or historical placement. And they convinced the majority of women they were right.

Now women of letters are in the process of doing the same thing. They are valuing women's writing, and creating a dominant space for that writing. In other words, they are creating the space for their own writing to be valued, at the expense of writers who do not share their backgrounds or their values.

But wait, now there's no time for us to rule dominant. We're not going to get the money, the prestige, and the satisfaction of doing all of this ourselves in the same way that men were able to. Because it's not just us, it's whole, huge populations who were also denied entry. And they, god damn it, have followed up our entry with demands for entry of their own. Before we even really got our hands on the controls. If only we could delay them for a while, convince them to just let us have it for a while, then it will totally be their turn . . .

The reason it's easy to say once we have equal power we will work toward inclusiveness for all is because that will not happen in our lifetime. But if we used the power we do have for the good of all rather than just for ourselves, we will not see the rewards we want. We will not get to live the way men have lived all of this time.

It is a failure of empathy to identify yourself only with those who resemble you. That is as narcissistic as working exclusively in your own self-interest.

The desire to focus on the change of the self, the empowerment of the self, is a symptom of a sense of inability to change the world, of a feeling of powerlessness. (It's easy to confuse the two, to think that because you are doing okay, the world must be as well.)

This sense of despair is caused by exhaustion. We tried hard to change society, to change the world, to build a space for women within the system. That did not fully work because it could not work. The system was built to keep us out. Now it's easier to focus on ourselves and on what we don't have rather than on what we do. It's also easier to focus on how we've been thwarted than to notice that there are other routes available to us. It's very easy to get distracted by our disappointments. To assume that the problem is our inability to get what we want, rather than that we want the wrong things. Not getting what you want is not oppression. In the same way that you, as an individual, doing well within the patriarchal system is not a political victory.

One of the reasons self-empowerment leads us to these places of dehumanization and exclusivity and narcissism is because we are still operating with patriarchal values and patriarchal definitions of what success is, what happiness is, what the meaning of life is.

Much of contemporary feminism uses the language of power. Girls need to be "empowered," women need to fight for "self-empowerment," "girl power," etc. There is little conversation about what that power is to be used for, because that is supposed to be obvious: whatever the girl wants.

But growing up in a system that measures success by money, that values consumerism and competition, that devalues compassion and community, these girls and women have already been indoctrinated into what to want. Without close examination, without conversion into a different way of thinking and acting, what that girl wants is going to be money, power, and, possibly, her continued subjugation, because a feminism that does not provide an alternative to the system will still have the system's values.

For centuries, the patriarchal system has defined happiness as having someone else subject to your will. You had someone else to hold all of your shit for you, so that you would not have to acknowledge its existence.

It's not that we don't have the power to create new lives and new forms of community. It's that if we do, we will not benefit from the patriarchal reward of power, which is what we have been taught to want. We have been taught that we will be happier with more money, we will be happier if we are the center of attention, we will be happier if we have a nuclear family and a supportive spouse. Self-empowerment would only allow us to do actual good if it came along with an interrogation of our desires and our definitions of happiness. Otherwise we'll continue to live in a world in which one group is empowered and another group is disempowered.

We have the power to do good, but that will not come to much as long as we define "what is good" as "what is good for me." According to this kind of thinking, creating a world in which I am welcomed and free is a superior goal to creating a world in which all are welcome and free.

Finding new modes of existing means rejecting the rewards that we've been promised for playing along.

It is only within the patriarchal structure that women have their freedoms curtailed. Moving beyond that structure means forgoing the rewards that structure doles out for participation. But it also gives you back your agency.

6

The Fights We Choose

The targets of feminism, particularly Internet feminism, are individual acts of misogyny. Once a questionable act is committed, both men and women are brought up for review and (if found lacking) punishment is doled out, usually in the form of an organized attempt to get the man or woman fired from his or her job.

In the past few years, watching this from the sidelines, I've seen the process play out for people accused of alleged rape and harassment, high-profile cases of unequal pay, misogynist statements by politicians, writers, and other men in power, a second wave feminist who was unfamiliar with the relatively new phrase "intersectional," feminist essays that did not adequately align with the particular feminist sensibilities of certain online commenters, an older man who made an awkward joke, and a rocket scientist who wore the wrong shirt to a press conference.

Names are called out, protests are organized, hashtags are circulated. The results are generally the same: either the figure doubles down on the unpopular position, or an institution, trying to avoid public humiliation or a boycott, quickly discards the offending individual and replaces them.

Much has already been written about "outrage culture," usually by potential targets. They claim we are living in a coddled culture, that women have lost their sense of humor, that the backlash to perceived misogyny is way out of proportion to the initial act. They call it "political correctness gone mad."

I don't really care about any of that. Whether this man was unjustly fired, whether this woman deserved the unhinged emails she received for weeks. In the grand scheme of things, a man facing outsized consequences for an unconscious and poorly considered deed or expression does not really compare to the day-to-day consequences women face for existing in public in a patriarchal society.

But my shrug is a problem. When I heard about Tim Hunt, a Nobel Prize–winning chemist who was removed from his post at a university because he told a bad joke taken out of context by someone online, I didn't really care. I felt that because he was an old white man, surely he had done other sexist things that merited his being fired, even if one joke shouldn't be enough to destroy a career. I believe my response was something along the lines of, "Another old fool, raised to believe women are inferior to men intellectually. It's now catching up to him." Just another dude, being a dude, feeling the repercussions of being a dude. The fact that a bunch of male scientists and commentators immediately began to shake their fists about "lynch mobs" and "political correctness gone mad" hardened my position that Hunt losing his job did not actually matter.

Eventually, my not caring started to bother me, particularly once I read the context of the joke. (Hunt had joked in a speech that women should not be allowed in the laboratory with men, because they are always falling in love with the men and getting distracted. The vital piece of information missing from this discussion was that this was how he met his wife, who was next to him at the time.) Socially awkward man makes a "take my wife . . . please" joke at a scientific function, it's heard by the wrong person, and suddenly he has no friends anywhere. The Royal

Society immediately distanced themselves, and
he was sacked in a matter of days.

The sequence of events revealed that there was
someone in the audience coiled and waiting to
lash out. Someone wanted and was ready to take
someone down. It is, in a way, understandable.
Women have faced a great deal of misogyny in
the sciences. A woman who has excelled in the
field has inevitably faced everything from unconscious discouragement in her education to the
jokey boys club atmosphere of the laboratory to a
lack of real mentoring to outright discrimination
when seeking employment or promotions. That
person is going to have, and rightly so, a lot of
rage built up over the span of her career.

But the audience member who started the
attack on Tim Hunt is not the only one coiled.
Consider the institutions who removed their support for Hunt without even a review of the circumstances. They must have seen this play out
in the past, the way a protest like this so quickly
becomes entrenched and how unwelcome "outrage" feminists have become to a nuanced conversation. There was Hunt's university, which
fired him without hesitation—again, because of a
bad joke—because they have seen protests get out
of control on campuses in the past and wanted to
nip this in the bud. Every woman who retweeted

the original attack on Hunt, every woman who immediately called for Hunt's head, they were all coiled and ready to believe the worst about someone, simply because the target was a straight, white, older man who worked in the sciences. Or, simply because he was a man. They felt sure enough of his guilt (and were ready enough to take someone down) without checking to make sure he said what his original attacker claimed.

Hunt's peers who used a thoughtless phrase ("lynch mob") to describe the actions of the feminist protestors, they had been waiting to lash out, too. More than a few of them probably knew that this could have happened to them just as easily if someone had had a phone set to record at an unguarded moment.

Revenge has become an official part of feminist policy. I can be blasé about a man losing his job and finding a lifetime of work dismissed all because he happened to tell a bad joke. As can a great number of women and feminist activists, which is why there has been so little push back on this cycle within the feminist community. There is a downside here. The longer we stay trapped in this destructive dynamic, the less we are using our energy for something constructive. We think we are doing something productive through these individual acts of revenge. And most of the feminist culture remains unconscious as to why this is a repeating pattern of behavior and why outrage culture feels so good.

We all keep a list buried deep within us, a list of every injustice, every indignity, every time we were rendered powerless and, instead of fighting back or speaking up, we did nothing. This is the list that powers outrage culture.

We forget to think critically about this list, to determine which incidents were the result of misogyny, which were the result of just bad luck or shit that happens, or maybe that some of this was actually our fault. Misdirected rage is not only destructive—because everyone has some and many are willing to fire where you say to aim—it is also foolish and embarrassing. Too little examination of your own list and you become that girl who sued the university that rejected her, saying it was affirmative action that filled the university with subpar minority students rather than her own painful mediocrity in grades, test scores, and activities. It's a convenient outlet, outrage. We use it to avoid the hard work of self-examination.

We also forget that other people have their own lists because of things we have done. People of other races, people from other countries, people of different sexualities, they have all had to deal with our stupid thoughtlessness, that thing we said or wrote, that shove we gave, or even just the way we looked at them, waiting for them to exhibit some sort of terrible behavior so that we could feel justified about expecting the worst from them. No one is perfectly enlightened. Even straight men have these lists, and a lot of those lists have valid entries.

The way we show up on other people's lists should give us insight into discriminating between what is thoughtless behavior and what is malicious behavior. There is a huge difference between them. The moment we think, say, or behave in a way that is, for example, racist, if that moment is willingly examined and not denied or shrugged off, it should help us understand where these beliefs come from.

What is the root of that stupid racist thought? Is it a pure expression of what you actually think or believe about this person and the group they belong to? Or do we take on so much influence from our society and our media (which are all fundamentally and institutionally racist, homophobic, xenophobic, and sexist) that there are unchecked corners of our mind where that influence has been spreading, unnoticed? We hide these moments because we are rightfully ashamed and we know what can come of them. Pretending those moments do not exist allows us to sit in judgment upon those who maybe have less control over their darker regions.

This is not to say individuals bear no responsibility for these moments of bias and hate. We do. It is our job, as citizens, to go out of our way to examine and understand this influence, and then undermine its power through education, consuming the culture produced by other groups, listening, and, above all, empathy. Understanding our own weakness should help us understand that the core of misogyny (and racism, and homophobia, etc.) lies not in the heart of the individual but in the way our society is structured. We should understand that going after misogyny individual by individual will be about as effective as someone calling you out for your own hidden prejudice. No matter how we try to cleanse ourselves, the core remains, until we who are willing to fight turn our focus from the distraction to the source.

We are not encouraged to do this hard work, because we are all spending too much time tending to our own lists. With everyone focused on their own outrage, it's difficult to create new patterns.

● ● ●

There is a difference between outrage and having standards. Outrage feminists are like the Furies, demanding an eye for an eye. Or an eye for an eyelash. A job for a joke. That need lives in all of us, and we're fucked if we feed it.

Standards of behavior, which, fine, can be labeled "political correctness" if you like, require that everyone live up to a certain expectation of humanity. If someone violates those standards in a serious way, through violence or outright hatred, that person should be set up for punishment. But if someone simply fails to live up to a certain expectation of humanity, then that person should be, not banished, but disagreed with. Their action should start a conversation. We, if we are going to demand a certain standard of behavior, should also meet that standard ourselves. Existing in a community means tolerating hard moments and allowing for other people's weaknesses, so that our hard moments are tolerated and our weaknesses are allowed.

We do not like to pay attention to how the casual demonization of white straight men follows the same pattern of bias and hatred that fuels misogyny, racism, and homophobia. It might not count as sexism because it does not have institutional power behind it, but it follows the same lazy thinking, easy scapegoating, and pleasurable anger that all other forms of hatred have.

My argument here is not that we need to protect men from this hatred. At its worst, this hatred is going to hurt feelings and create anger and resentment. My argument is that we need to protect ourselves from falling into this lazy trap. It feels good to be antagonistic, to create an "I'm-in, you're-out" kind of club. But that way of thinking, speaking, and writing is totally devoid of value. Dismissing someone for being a white, straight male lowers us to the level of an ideologue. When this white male scapegoat becomes code for boring, privileged, and mediocre, it means we are no longer thinking, we are simply repeating stereotypes. It's reductive in the same way that all stereotypes are reductive.

We also have to think about what kind of intellectual environment we want to live in. An environment where we strong-arm dissidence and varied opinion is an environment devoid of possibility and dynamism. With the feminist audience putting so much emphasis on proper language and terminology, with so little regard for the legitimacy and power of the ideas beneath the surface, feminist discourse has become shallow. And when even minor disagreements can be exaggerated as attacks and abuse, this does not allow much space for writers to work out complicated ideas in public.

We might think it preferable never to be challenged, but it turns out surrounding yourself only with people who agree with you leads to degraded thought. Using the excuse that men have controlled and dominated the conversation for centuries does not justify using their methods to try to wrench control our way.

We need a sharp-edged feminism that does not shy away from the big battles we have yet to face. If we want to create a better world, we need the foundations to be different, not to be the same foundations patriarchy was built on. But this is the sticky problem that it is going to be hard to circumvent: most women are not fundamentally better than most men. Unless the conversation moves away from the mire in which it's become stuck—away from the outrage cycle that feels so good but is devoid of substance—we risk changing the world in an interior-designer kind of way. The basic structure is the same, but aren't the new curtains nice?

• • •

What does outrage actually accomplish? There was probably a moment when calling out the actions of some guy opened up a conversation, something along the lines of: How can we be more supportive of women in science? But that moment has passed. Now the only people allowed to talk at all after something like the Hunt affair are the women who suffered similar stories. They cluster together, tell each other how much they've had to overcome, and threaten retribution against anyone who dares to challenge their version of events.

Outrage is now met with quick fixes—one person fired, another person driven from Twitter, another person forced into an insincere public apology—and people are learning not to speak up. Not telling the sexist joke does not mean the underlying sexism no longer exists. People just get better at hiding their prejudices. Making racial slurs socially unacceptable has obviously not done anything to create a less racist world, as evidenced by the brutal slayings of black men and women by the police force. It's unlikely that banning all sexist jokes, then, will do anything to create a better environment for women. Quick fixes are not enough, political correctness that is not matched with institutional change is ineffective, and disproportionate punishment does nothing but create resentment and fear.

Responding to our own personal outrage keeps misogyny on a personal level. It keeps us going person by person, trying to root out any hidden psychological damage, any deep hatred or mommy issues. The outward expression of misogyny is the distraction; the individual misogynist is the symptom, not the cause. Taking out one individual at a time does not decrease the amount of misogyny in the world. The system we live in, a system that rewards competition and violence, a system that devalues compassion and care, will keep spitting out misogynists until the system itself is addressed.

We move away from outrage culture when we accept that there is no way to win this fight we're all engaged in. We cannot create a safe world by dealing with misogyny on an individual basis. It is our entire culture, the way it runs on money, rewards inhumanity, encourages disconnection and isolation, causes great inequality and suffering, that's the enemy. That is the only enemy worth fighting.

Fighting against the entire structure, though, means that we will probably not see true success in our lifetime. And progress might be so slow that we rarely feel it.

Outrage culture, despite being unproductive, if not entirely counter-productive, feels good because at least there appears to be a chance of winning. If we can vanquish one foe, if we can take down one man with sexism in his heart, then we have improved the world, one tiny bit. It feels like an accomplishment. But another person will just take his place. And perhaps this person will better know how to control the external manifestations of his internal hatred.

This system is shit, and it is against us. That is why we need to be cunning about where we put our intellectual energy. Wasting it on fighting Twitter bros and calling for the execution of harmless old men is not an efficient use of our time, energy, and resources.

7

Men Are Not Our Problem

If I may interrupt my train of thought for just a moment to direct my attention to any men who might be reading this book.

Maybe you picked up my manifesto because you too have some problems with feminism. Maybe those problems are sincere. Maybe you philosophically disagree with current feminist thought; maybe you genuinely support the basic tenets of feminism but are confused by how those tenets are currently being expressed. Maybe you've read Firestone and Dworkin and dealt with the feelings and thoughts they evoked. Maybe you've sorted through your own fear of weakness and vulnerability; maybe you've examined the ways you have in the past projected those feelings onto women. Maybe you've dealt with your discomfort with femininity; maybe

you have given space in your life to softness and
beauty and love.

Or maybe you tell yourself you are enlightened and sensitive but really it's just that you are
uncomfortable with women acting like they are
autonomous human beings. Maybe you want a
woman writer to tell you it's okay to think women
are stupid, illogical idiots and that feminism is
the embarrassing farce you deeply need it to be.
Maybe you are looking for any excuse available
not to take women seriously.

Probably you are somewhere in between. Either way, it's possible you have some questions
or concerns with what I've written here, and you
would like me to address these for you.

If so, this is my response: Take that shit somewhere else. I am not interested. You as a man are
not my problem. It is not my job to make feminism easy or understandable to you. It is not my
job to nurture and encourage your empathy, it is
not my job to teach you how to deal with women
being human beings.

And don't take that shit to other women either.
It's not their job. Your lack of enlightenment is not
our problem. Figure it out. Do the reading, feel
your own feelings, don't take them to someone
else. Men have to do this work on their own and
for each other. You cannot ask women to spend

the next century carrying the burden of your discomfort and confusion. Do your own fucking work, gentlemen.

I understand that men are going to have to go through a difficult time. They're going to have to do all of the self-examination and seeking they've spent centuries avoiding doing. They're going to have to find new ways of living and being on the planet. Women have a huge head start on them, and they're going to do all they can to avoid going through this process.

Your first encounter with feminism should make you uncomfortable. It has to break through all of the messages you've been indoctrinated with. You'll have to experience regret for your behavior, and you will have to acknowledge all the ways you've been consciously and unconsciously misogynistic during your lifetime. One way to avoid that discomfort is to ask women to reassure you that you are one of the good ones. To perform your sensitivity. It's manipulative. Another way to avoid that discomfort is to sit alone with your dark thoughts about what is wrong with feminists.

I just want to be clear that I don't give a fuck about your response to this book. Do not email me, do not get in touch. Deal with your own shit for once.

• • •

Now. Where were we?

Men take up a lot of space in our lives, but also
in our heads. They've been so instilled as the
"authority" in our society that we recreate that
authority as a specter in our imagination. It's
the male gaze internalized, except it is not only
about sexuality but the observation of all aspects
of our lives. In the same way we anticipate, even
unconsciously, men's responses to our physical
appearance, judging by their standards whether
or not we look sexy or pretty when we look in
the mirror, we can anticipate men's responses to
the way we behave, the way we speak, the choices
we make about how to live our lives. Our society
so values masculine modes of life and masculine
ways of seeing and judging, rewarding those who
fall into line, that we internalize this process.
Men in real life reinforce this by observing and
commenting on our behavior and our choices. It
is easy to mistake the degree of their importance.

But for all the space men take up in our imaginations, most of it is space we give them. We in-
vite them in and forget to usher them out. Even

in feminist discourse, the male audience is always presupposed and catered to.

Take, for example, the idea that feminists should present a united front, because any squabbling or dissension bolsters our enemies. Our enemies are simply the members of the male audience we've created in our heads.

I've seen this repeatedly in the pro-choice movement, both in person and online. Many women who have had abortions in the United States find the experience excruciating and confusing. They are often told by feminists that abortion is not a big deal. The party line is that the procedure causes a little discomfort, and then after you may feel sad but mostly just relieved.

Then they have the abortion, which can be very painful for some, and which can be followed by real grieving. When you're told that everything is fine and your experience is one in which nothing is fine, it can be difficult to reconcile that. Particularly when, in the United States, abortion clinics do not offer much in the way of counseling services, and the lack of insurance coverage for the procedure means the already expensive visit will become even more expensive if one wants medical pain relief during the abortion.

And yet when such women have spoken up about their difficult experiences, they have been asked to stay quiet. For the sake of the cause. Any ambivalence could be seized upon by our pro-life enemies, who could use it as an excuse to "protect" us from the damaging effects of abortion. Never mind the fact that our pro-life enemies have a long history of just making shit up about abortion and don't need our help to do so. It causes cancer, it causes PTSD, it causes infertility . . . They have that zone covered.

This idea that women or feminists should appear as a monolith seems to spring from the idea that a show of strength will allow us to overcome our enemies. We must be unified, we must be in control, we must not criticize the movement.

What this says, though, is that what our "enemies" think of us is more important than our own integrity. The idea that we should act more like them—as the political right operates often as a monolith in order to win battles—is a similarly misguided notion. It sacrifices a vision of a better future for the sake of feeling triumphant in the present.

Besides, though softness, vulnerability, nuance, compassion, and care may be devalued under the current system, they are absolutely vital qualities that we should not be ashamed of. Our first responsibility should be to take care of each other, as the system under which we all live will certainly not take care of us. We cannot do that if we see criticism as an attack or as a sign of weakness.

A conversation about how something should go, what a movement's goals should be, is not "squabbling." Disagreement and criticism are absolutely necessary if a situation is going to improve. And if people are being legitimately hurt, they have the right to voice that hurt and have their voices heard. To deny them audience simply because it is inconvenient, or because of worries of how that complaint will be heard by people outside the movement, is foolish. After all, people not given a voice within a movement will go looking for a place to be heard. Every human being has the right to be recognized as such.

It's not only male disapproval that is a problem. Male approval can be a hindrance as well. We are taught, as women, that whether or not we have value as human beings depends on what men think of us. Whether or not a woman is worthy of love is determined by men.

This system can use love and romance as a form of oppression and control. Certain behaviors and characteristics are deemed lovable or unlovable. Women act out this oppression by tailoring their behavior and characteristics to these rules.

Under the system, love is simply another thing to work and compete for. And the stakes are high, because romantic love isn't just how we give meaning to our lives, it's how we organize society. Couples cohabitate, share money, and they procreate.

Even with the rise of single motherhood, both in the number of women embarking on it and in its social acceptability, our society is organized so firmly around romantic love that there are very few options between raising a child as a couple (if the couple remains together, that arrangement will probably be the nuclear family model) and raising a child on your own. Single motherhood in a time of economic precarity means absorbing all financial, emotional, and physical risks on your own. Western societies continue to strip out most of their state welfare programs, but the problem is more pernicious than that.

We wait for love to redeem us. For straight girls, that means, despite all of our talk about independence and empowerment, the goals of self-empowerment are often pursued to make ourselves in better competitive shape on the romantic market.

For proof of this, we only need to look at our options if we choose to live outside of the romantic structure. For the most part, if you reject not only the idea of marriage but also of couplehood, your only viable choice for living is a solitary existence. Because the vast majority of women look to their love lives ultimately to organize their lives, to induct them into motherhood, to tell them where and how to live, if you try to stake out a life outside of that, you will spend much of your time alone.

Which is why if you decide to have a child outside of marriage, the responsibility of that child is yours alone. There are no (or very, very few) communal living spaces, there are no parenting contracts with non-romantic partners. Unless you have the money to substitute the care provided by you with bought care—from nannies to housekeepers—you are on your own.

The question is what this does to heterosexual women, who must rely on men, then, to organize their lives—unless they are prepared for a life of spinsterhood. (Even "spinsterhood"—in this era celebrated by slightly older unmarried women, who experience it more as a pre-couple stage of independence—is usually presumed to precede eventually being part of a couple.)

Marriage has survived decades of attacks by

feminist and queer thinkers, who have noted everything from the disturbing symbolic meaning of marriage—that women are property to be handed over from father to husband—to the way it often improves the lives of men at the expense of the health, career, and happiness of women. Their work is vitally important, but I won't be repeating it here.

I'm more concerned with the anticipation of marriage, of how that changes feminism's goals and practice. Because there are so few alternatives to romantic love as your life's organizing principle, other than self-reliance, there is a pressure from adolescence on to make yourself lovable and fuckable to your desired potential mate.

Take beauty, for example. Beauty is still strongly linked to ideas of lovability. One way that feminists have tried to deal with the pressure of finding themselves on the binary of beautiful and ugly, fuckable and unfuckable, is to try to expand what qualifies as beautiful. That becomes the feminist campaign, to see fat bodies as beautiful, to see non-white bodies as beautiful, to see differently abled bodies as beautiful.

But beauty in our culture is not only linked to physical features. Notions of acceptability are involved. Which is why we are constantly reminded by the media that women who make themselves "too much," either too ambitious or too independent or too educated, will find themselves unlovable.

The only reasonable option, then, is to reject notions of beauty and ugliness altogether. Not to expand ideas of beauty, but to shut them down. To reject the labels. To reject the judgment.

This doesn't require a kind of second wave throwback to rejecting bras and fashion and make-up and haircuts done by professionals. (Although a year or two of being not only rejected, but not even acknowledged long enough to be rejected by the male gaze never hurt anyone.) But simply that notions of beauty, of acceptability, of lovability and fuckability should be divorced from our sense of value. The only way this will ever be true is if romantic love is demoted from being the central feature of our lives.

(And because love under our system is a competition in the way that money and career is a competition, these beauty standards, these rules of behavior, these notions of acceptability, are often maintained and supported by other women. In the same way that women who profit from the patriarchy will help keep it in place, women who profit from these standards in love and sexuality will also help keep them in place.)

The problem here is not the individual woman

trying to be beautiful or lovable. Girls posting selfies on Instagram are not killing feminism, nor are the girls on Tumblr writing about the beauty of bodies that society often tells them are ugly. The problem is that feminism has offered women so few alternatives to give their lives meaning and value. We have not created the infrastructure, nor even the imagination, to allow women to live different kinds of lives, lives outside of the romantic complex.

Because while marriage as an institution has been widely criticized by feminists, we mistook the criticisms to mean relationships just needed renegotiating. That while marriage as a whole was obviously problematic, an individual marriage could be negotiated to be more egalitarian and supportive. But it should not be up to an individual woman to undo centuries, millennia of oppression and control. It is not the existence of love that is the problem, it is its primacy. It is the coupling of romantic love with not only emotional but social and material reward.

Feminists do not have to shut themselves off from the possibility of romantic love. But we should question the privileging of romantic love over all other forms of love, from familial to friendship to societal. We should also question what is required of us in order to be loved, and the way the possibility of love and sex and family is dangled in front of women as a way of keeping them in line—and the way women are all too eager to internalize this method of control.

It's our imaginations that are stunted here. I have read many books, I have watched many movies, written or directed by women, where the author demonstrates to the audience that the female character has value by having all of the male characters fall in love with her. Even if she is too traumatized, too hard, been through too much shit to be in a relationship, the male characters moon around her, expressing their feelings, telling her they're here for her when she's "ready," they look at her with such longing and feeling.

The stories we tell reveal what it is we value. And traditional feminist stories, of love, of self-empowerment, of material success, reveal that we still look to men to bestow value upon us. Either through using their metrics of employment and money or by looking to them to tell us we are lovable. There are so few stories and ideas about how to live outside of these systems and still feel and be acknowledged as valuable and respectable. If there is going to be a celebrated female loner in our culture, then she had better behave like a male loner: financially independent, sexually voracious, childfree, and without any ties to community or society.

We have to imagine something before we can build the infrastructure that will allow it to exist. We have failed here on both fronts: in imagination and in reality. Our great weirdos, from Emily Dickinson to Simone Weil to Coco Chanel, are seen as outliers, as not relevant to the way we think through what we want out of life. It's the same way we dismiss radical feminist writers like Dworkin and Firestone. Dworkin is unhinged, Firestone is too eccentric to be taken seriously.

Feminism has the power to transform culture, not just respond to it. The reason why we don't transform it is because the majority of us benefit from organizing society around romantic love. We benefit not only emotionally, but financially, socially, and materially as well. There have always been women on the margins, the unfuckable and unlovable spinsters, the poor, the sex workers, the pre–legal gay marriage lesbians. They have always been vulnerable, outside the male protection that the fuckable feminists enjoy. And they've often been scapegoated and ignored by feminists. Maybe because the societal rejects remind feminists how easy it is to fall out of favor. And how dependent they still remain on men.

Just because we benefit from something, that does not make it a social good. It also doesn't mean it is the best we can do. If you want to inspire real change, it has to begin in the imagination; you have to give people the chance to imagine a better way of living. In that way, the feminist response to love and marriage has failed.

I have more questions than answers. I do not know how this all is supposed to go. I'm fine with that, you should never listen to anyone who says they have it all figured out. They are either lying or they want something from you.

No one individual, no one gender, no one race, no one nationality has the right to create reality for everyone else. The era of domination has to be replaced with an era of collaboration, not segmentation. The only way this is possible is if we come together with a sense of our shared obligations, not an inflated sense of what we deserve. And simply because one individual or group is unable to leave their sense of entitlement behind is no excuse for adopting an "I'll just take what I can get" attitude. The way to fight selfishness is not more selfishness.

There's a difference between something not being our problem and something not being our responsibility. Men are not our problem, but they are our responsibility.

The difference lies in the actions taken. It is not our job to escort men into a new awareness. We do not need to become missionaries, converting them to our version of enlightenment.

Though conversion, in a missionary sense, is tempting for many reasons. We get to control the outcome. We think for some reason that we know best what it is men need, and we think we are giving them a gift by convincing them. And we do try to convince them—those of us who fall into the habit of thinking of men as our problems— that we know best what they should be like.

But with conversion, what we want is for men to think like us, to think we are right, to behave in ways that give us our ideal partners, our ideal brothers, our ideal sons, our ideal colleagues. When men are our problem, we are ultimately thinking of ourselves, and how men relate to us. We try to manage men, constantly, with the way we talk about and to them, with the way we reward or punish them with companionship or solitude, in the stories we tell about them—much in the same way men have thought of women as being their problem for a very long time now.

When men are our responsibility rather than our problem, we don't get a say in how their experimentation turns out. We don't get to pretend like we know best. We are not the experts of masculinity.

That does not mean we check out entirely from the process. We give them the space to experiment, to fuck up, to think it through. Traditional modes of masculinity, fatherhood, partnership are being rethought, and it is our responsibility to allow the patriarchy to unmake itself and create something new. We can create something new side by side, without one group trying to dominate or control the other.

Giving space means listening more than speaking, not punishing, with word or deed behavior, that makes us uncomfortable unless it is actually doing real physical or psychic harm. It means allowing for the uncertainty of the outcome. This is what we have been demanding of men since feminism's beginning: that they allow us this space for ourselves. The fact that they have done an imperfect job does not mean we should deny them the same grace. When I say that feminism has the power and the responsibility to reimagine and recreate thought and society, I do not mean women. I do not mean, "Women must lead us to the new Jerusalem." It is the philosophy that powers feminism—that men and women are equal in value and in strength—that will allow us to reimagine the world together, in a way that is beneficial to all and not only for ourselves. Men can and must participate in this project.

For that to happen, we must reimagine our relationships to and with men, as well as our ideas of who men are. It's not only our imaginations that are colonized by desire, men's are as well. They too are infected by the ideas of who we want them to be.

Let us create a world of cooperation and fraternity, and leave behind the notion that one group creates the world on behalf of everyone else.

8

Safety Is a Corrupt Goal

Women have suffered. It is nearly impossible to ever give full witness to the way women throughout history have suffered physically, psychologically, emotionally from living within a patriarchal system.

And there's no need to spend time restating those ways here. If you're here in this book, you know. We all know.

There has, perhaps, been too much time spent chronicling those trials in feminist writing. We want to make our point, obviously. We want to get it across to people that we have suffered in a multitude of ways and that we continue to suffer. Part of the chronicling is simply to provide company to women, to let them know that they are not crazy for thinking something they've been told is good for them is actually bad for them, to let them know their cognitive dissonance has a source. It's a way of piercing through the fantasy that the system under which we live is not oppressive, and showing that that system is indeed causing harm.

But then there's that other motivation, the desire to make the person oppressing us stop oppressing us. And so we point out, hey, this is my bruise, this is my wound, this thing you did caused it. Please stop.

The suffering is a fact. What is important now is what we do with it. It doesn't take much time to look around the geopolitical scene and see how one group's suffering is used as a way to justify the suffering of others. It's important that we use our suffering as a way to build empathy, which requires vulnerability, rather than as an excuse never to be vulnerable again.

There is a temptation when one has suffered to say that one has suffered *enough*. As in, no more. The temptation is to go about creating a form of protection, to insist that you be kept safe from further harm. "Harm" under these conditions becomes nebulous; anything from threats of violence to reminders of past hurts to even experiencing discomfort can meet the criteria of "harmful."

Safety is about control. In order to feel safe,

things have to be made predictable. And the only way in life to make something predictable is to control the outcome. Whether that is through manipulation or abuse, it's an unethical impingement on other people's freedom.

There is a big difference between safety and peace. Safety is a kind of surface level cleanliness, where outward behavior is the most important thing. It's like the city that brags about how safe and clean its streets are, and meanwhile the jails are filled with the homeless and the poor and the mentally ill, and littering gets you publicly whipped.

That's very different from a city that is peaceful, where social programs address poverty and mental illness, where housing is provided for those without, where crime rates are low because of civil community policing.

Currently, safety for women means strict prison sentencing for men, prioritizing revenge over rehabilitation. Despite all the information we have about what a hellscape the American prison system is, many feminists demand jail time for offenses and advocate for hate crime designations which necessarily lengthen sentences.

Safety for women means designating certain language as hate speech and moving toward silencing it with petitions and protests, rather than countering uncivil speech with thoughtful, civil speech.

This is about control. To feel safe, you need to control what the people around you are going to say and do. This is not achieved by going after the root causes of violence. This is not even achieved by working to slowly improve social conditions. It is achieved through silence and disappearance, by moving the offending object or person out of sight.

I am not talking about prioritizing the rights of people to commit violence or say shitty things. This is a conversation about what kind of world we want to live in. Do we want to live in a world that is safe? Do we want to push the homeless out of our cities and call that a victory over poverty? "Look, all the people living on the streets are gone, we did a super good job conquering that problem!" Or do we want to do the very hard work of recognizing and addressing the actual causes of harm to women?

Safety is a short-term goal and it is unsustainable. Eventually, the unaddressed causes will find new ways of manifesting themselves as problems. Pull up the dandelions all you want, but unless you dig up that whole goddamn root it's just going to keep showing back up.

Peace, however, is something worth fighting for.

• • •

For centuries, the safety of women has been used as a propaganda tool. If you want to commit an atrocity, talk about how the people you want to destroy are a threat to your women. This has been used to push everything from anti-immigration laws (with posters of white women being mauled and handled by scary black hands) to the invasion of Afghanistan. We should not forget that many feminists supported that war because of the Taliban's oppression of women. Rather than improving the lives of Afghan women, we killed a large number of them and made their daily lives even less secure and more terrifying.

We fought for the "right" of women to join the military, and we celebrated winning the right of women to fight on the front lines in combat as a feminist victory. It's not only in our name that others are fighting, we are now using our own safety as an excuse to pick up guns, invade other countries, and kill their inhabitants.

We should be careful, then, when we invoke this idea of women's safety; we should be aware of the history of how this has been used to justify violence.

It's troubling that we look to a patriarchal system like the criminal justice complex, which causes the suffering of many and thrives on injustice to the poor, to address problems of safety for women. Our criminal justice system, after all, is geared toward revenge and punishment, not rehabilitation and prevention.

Of course, the criminal justice system has failed us for years. It has failed to take seriously accusations of rape, domestic violence, sexual harassment, and abuse. It has punished us as often, if not more often, than it has punished those who hurt us. We have also seen how the system has hurt our men, particularly our poor and black men. We've seen how it's executed them, tortured them, and sent them away from us for years for minor offenses. Is our answer really going to be found within that system? If that system suddenly starts taking violence against women seriously, without addressing the other injustices it creates, can we actually consider that system "reformed"? Do we really want to push the bodies of even more (poor and black) men into a system that is designed to destroy them?

There was a court case a while back that was like a lot of other court cases throughout time. It was a he said, she said. She said he abused her, he said he did not. There was no physical evidence, so the court case was built exclusively on testimony. Except the defense did have evidence, they had emails from the woman to the man expressing love and desire for him, emails sent after the incident in question. In court she said the sex was not consensual. In the emails she said she loved the sex they had.

There are a lot of reasons why women might send emails like that to their abuser. For one, it is a way of trying to get their abuser to stop abusing them. Please stop hurting me, this is how much I love you.

At any rate, the judge dismissed the case, as he should have. The emails opened up a world of doubt regarding the testimony of the accuser, the huge possibility that this accusation was an act of revenge against a man who spurned her. Feminists were outraged. Women should be believed, they said. Women do not lie about these kinds of things. They should have celebrated, or at least tolerated, the decision, as it was a civil rights victory. For the man, yes, but it was still a victory. The man, of Indian descent (not white), did not get railroaded into jail on nothing but one white woman's word. We should not forget that a white woman's accusation against a man of color has caused lynchings and the imprisonment of the innocent in the past.

After all, women do lie about these kinds of things. They have all sorts of reasons to lie, from getting revenge to getting attention. Some women are terrible. We should not forget this. And we should not insist that women don't lie as a way of bolstering their credibility, because every false accusation immediately undermines *our* credibility for saying so.

Feminists should have supported the judge's decision, because the goal should be justice. Not fake justice, not injustice where a woman's testimony is weighed more heavily than a man's simply because of her gender.

"BUT," I can hear you cry, "there are men who will never believe women when they accuse men of rape and abuse. There are men who think the worst of women, who think that women have sex with men all the time just to accuse them of rape later and destroy their lives. How else are we ever going to convince them?"

Let me repeat what I have stated earlier: Men are not our fucking problem. You can't overcompensate for some men's problems with women by insisting on our purity and innocence. The way we deal with other people's inhumanity is to insist on our humanity, not by insisting we are somehow a better, more honest version of human. That requires admitting to the shitty things that some women do, the violence they commit, the lies they tell to get what they want. Our job is not to convince anyone of anything. That is another form of control: telling someone what they want to hear to get them to believe what we want them to believe. Our job is to act like humans.

We need to be aware of our desire for revenge, as discussed earlier. This truly is perhaps the first era in which women's claims against men are taken seriously, where there is a chance for action. We need to be careful what we do with that possibility.

In a culture that thrives on outrage, that has been primed by its constant retelling of our history of suffering to respond strongly to new violations, there can be a lack of mercy and restraint. You see this playing out in social media behavior. A man is accused of abusing a woman, and the immediate response is to try to get that person fired. Even if the problem was personal and had nothing to do with his workplace. A professor is accused of abusing a romantic partner? Petition the university to get that man fired. A doctor is accused? Blacklist that motherfucker, go after his livelihood.

This is not justice, and it does not create a safe environment for women. The protesters say their focus is on protecting women, but they are not acting in a way that supports that claim.

What they are doing is looking for one man to carry the weight of our entire history, to make up for all of the men who hurt us and escaped punishment. This is revenge. With revenge, nothing will ever be enough. We don't want understanding, we want to destroy lives. If that were not the case, then when an accusation was made against a man, women who called themselves feminists would argue for restraint, would allow the system chosen to address the accusation to decide what should be done. If that system is broken, like the criminal justice system, they would make it their goal to reform that system to promote rehabilitation and reconciliation over punishment. Or they would work to design a different way of addressing interpersonal issues.

It's understandable that women would not trust the criminal justice system to deal reasonably and decisively with women's issues. But the answer is not vigilantism. Nor is it doing us any good to insist on outsized punishments, becoming an Old Testament Yahweh, causing floods in response to blasphemy or destroying cities in response to unapproved sexual behavior.

When we talk about women's safety as being the top priority, what we are talking about is separating women out from society, not creating space for them within society. We are talking about creating methods of control and manipulation. We are saying that the world needs to be reorganized not around fairness and peace, but around our particular needs and desires. If we continue to define our group's identity by what has been done to us, we will continue to be object rather than subject.

Once safety becomes the goal, once we have reached the fed-up point of *enough*, then we start scanning our environments for threats. It's easy, from this position, to confuse irritations for full-on assaults. Friends can look like enemies when you are on high alert. And calling out for safety and protection can be a way of refusing to take responsibility for your own situation.

Everything is more complicated than anyone wants to admit. When there is a crime or a confrontation or even simply a disagreement, one way to simplify it is to label one person as the aggressor and the other person as the victim. There are advantages to being labeled the victim. You are listened to, paid attention to. Sympathy is bestowed upon you. Once you have been declared a victim, you are allowed to rest, you are given time to recover. Everything you do is brave. You can be sympathetic as to why people might want to be in that victimhood space.

It's why so many people make up stories of victimization, like people writing memoirs claiming to have survived the Holocaust, white girls from the suburbs claiming to be inner-city gang members, white men pretending to be Native American, mothers making their children sick just to get attention at the hospital. Part of the reasoning for why women would never lie about being victimized is that the scrutiny is so brutal—why would anyone put themselves through it? Except that we know why. We know because so many people have lied in the same way before.

The role of victim is easier if you can claim association with a historically victimized group, like women. This clarifies the aggressor's otherwise murky intentions—the aggressor hates women. Otherwise, he would not have hit/raped/spoken badly against/thought badly of/stolen from this particular woman.

A crime, an assault, a difficult encounter are

interactions. Sometimes it is clear there is a random victim with a clear aggressor. Sometimes someone picks your pocket. Other than obliviousness, the victim is not guilty of anything and did not participate in his own victimization. Sometimes it's more complicated. Sometimes you are a tourist in a poor country wearing an expensive watch or carrying a fancy bag. If that watch or bag is taken from you, that's more complicated. It's not that this person deserved to be the victim of this crime, but it is more complicated. There are factors that must be considered, low levels of personal responsibility that must be confronted, otherwise a seed of hatred sets in. If you're a white, well-off North American in, let's say, Latin America, and this happens to you, it is easy to say, "These are dirty, criminal people in this country," without confronting how you participated in this situation.

Something similar is happening when we claim that people who hurt us hate women. Some do, sure, but misogyny is not the inevitable origin of these interactions. But if we're in high-alert mode, even minor disagreements start to look like assaults. You see this of course most clearly online, where everyone is on high alert all the time. A man (who yes should probably have kept his mouth shut anyway) questions a claim by a woman, and suddenly he is a misogynist. It allows the woman writer to dismiss his question out of hand. Not only that, questioning itself becomes a kind of attack.

This also allows interpersonal problems to become misogyny-motivated crimes. Women, who often feel powerless in the romantic realm, can use this frame to absolve themselves of any wrongdoing. Of say, just being a jerk in a relationship or on a date. If things don't go the way she wants, there's a way of understanding this failure as originating in the man's clear, unprocessed hatred of women, rather than, "This is a pretty normal way men and women manage to hurt each other when intimacy creates vulnerability."

Labeling aggressors as misogynists also gives us an easy way of understanding what has happened to us. It's not about *us*, it's our womanhood. But beware of easy stories and self-serving narratives. The true misogynists, the real predators, those are what they are really using against us.

Simply put, being alive, and being a participant in the world, fucks you up. Prioritizing your safety, or your group's safety, over creating an environment that is safer for all, is a refusal to participate in the world. It's saying, "This world is not good enough, and until it bends itself to my will, I'll have nothing to do with it."

The refusal to participate, to allow yourself to be hurt and shocked and fucked up, is a betrayal to the people with whom you claim alliance. Women. If you want to create a better world and a better existence for your people, you must participate in the imperfect world that exists now. Besides, what would be the meaning of all of that suffering if all we did with it was use it as an excuse to cause the suffering of others? It would all be for nothing. Let's take what we've suffered and learn something from it.

9

Where We Go from Here

You are not doing feminism wrong.

You are not ruining things for women, you are not betraying your sisters. The choices you make on a daily basis—your haircut, your diet, which petition you sign, the opinions you voice, which television show you either pay for or download illegally—are not destroying the world.

But just as much, you are not saving the world. You are not heroically making the world safer for women with your haircut, your diet, the petitions you sign, the opinions you voice, or the television show you either pay for or download illegally.

For too long, feminism has been moving away from being about collective action and collective imagination, and toward being a lifestyle. Lifestyles do not change the world.

• • •

One thing the patriarchal system under which we live definitely wants you to believe is that you are on your own. Independence and freedom are what you wanted, right? So independent, you swing toward fragility and loneliness. So free, you exist in a blank space with no guideposts or reference points.

Feminism can and should be an alternative to this isolation. It should be a way of creating alternatives to the way we live.

We have a very serious barrier here: we want our lives to be comfortable.

Now is an interesting time to start a revolution, as no one's life is truly comfortable. With increasing political, economic, and social instability, everyone's life is vulnerable to falling apart at any moment. So why not do something creative with that instability, rather than simply trying to shore up what is destined to fall?

Stop trying to maintain order amid the chaos. Stop trying to save you and yours first. Terrible atrocities have been committed in the name of "protecting my family."

• • •

We need to define what it is we value, how we express that value, and what we ask society to value in us.

Money is currently how we express value, particularly through our unconscious association between income and worth. As in, if someone is financially struggling, they must not be producing anything of value. If someone is financially successful, they must be producing work of tremendous value. But also: if I am not being paid for my work, that work must not be valuable.

In order to dismantle our patriarchal, capitalistic, consumerist society, we have to go after these belief systems in ourselves and in others. We must stop telling each other stories that equate money with value. We must imagine a world where value is expressed with things like love and care.

We also must stop going up to the patriarchy and asking it to value us. We must admit to ourselves that success under this system is suspect.

We have to understand our power, that we are not at the mercy of this culture. We are participants of it. We can shape it. But that requires work, not simply commentary. Stop reacting to the moving parts. Lay your attack at the machinery itself.

We must lay claim to the culture, occupy it. We must remember that our world does not have to be this way. We do not have to reward exploitation, we do not have to support the degradation of the planet, of our souls, of our bodies. We can resist. We must stop thinking so small.

We must reclaim our imaginations. We have been limited by the patriarchal imagination, infected by it. We see only as far as they see.

We must begin again to see beyond the structures we've been given. The way we order our lives, our homes, our work, our souls—our worldviews must be reimagined in wholly new ways. This is more important than ever before.

And if you are not up for this, if you just want your life to be comfortable, if you just want to make your money and watch your shows and do as well as you can in this lifetime, then admit it to yourself. You are not a feminist. Just stand in your truth and get it over with.

But I hope you change your mind. Because we need you.

Author's Note

I am deeply indebted to the work of writers like Sarah Schulman, Emil Cioran, Dubravka Ugrešić, Shlomo Sand, Virginie Despentes, R. I. Moore, Franco "Bifo" Berardi, Isabell Lorey, bell hooks, Simone de Beauvoir, Angela McRobbie, Mattilda Bernstein Sycamore, Jacqueline Rose, Diane di Prima, Michelle Cliff, Helen Garner, Laura Kipnis, Maria Tatar, Emma Goldman, Marina Warner, Eva Illouz, Bruce Benderson, Hélène Cixous, Mark Simpson, Sonia Faleiro, Simone Weil, Stephanie Coontz, St. Teresa of Ávila, Julia Kristeva, Sandra Rodríguez Nieto, and many others. Read their books.

Photograph by Chuck Kuan

A Note About the Author

Jessa Crispin is the editor and founder of the
online magazine *Bookslut* and the online literary
journal *Spolia*. She is the author of *The Dead Ladies
Project* and *The Creative Tarot,* and has written for
numerous leading publications, including *The New
York Times, The Guardian, The Washington Post,*
and others.